"Nothing can ever be like sm[...] experience. Nothing can eve[...] summers, the early mornings, the wafting of airplane exhaust, and the sound of engines roaring as you step out into the cold air, into harm's way—to the smell of smoke and the endless beauty and incredible drama of the western mountains of America. *Jason Ramos brings all that alive in this book.*

Smokejumpers today are carrying on a long tradition of service to our government, to the environment and to saving lives. It is vitally important that this tradition continue. Initial attack has become old news these days, where too often fires are left to burn. Too often these become conflagrations which destroy lives, property and the environment, costing tens of millions to finally contain. This book will give you an inside look at the world of smokejumping, and an intimate understanding of how exceptional—and vital—the smokejumping program is to the future of the American west."

—BILL FURMAN, *CEO, Greenbrier Companies, Inc., Smokejumper NCSB '62–'67*

"Jason Ramos weaves personal experiences, smokejumper history, fire science, and fire operations into a fascinating book. It is a must-read for all firefighters as well as any American who lives or recreates in or near wildfire-prone areas."

—LARRY LUFKIN, *son of Francis Lufkin, Smokejumper NCSB '40, '46, '48–'50, MSO '42–'44*

SMOKEJUMPER

SMOKEJUMPER

A MEMOIR BY ONE OF AMERICA'S
MOST SELECT AIRBORNE FIREFIGHTERS

JASON A. RAMOS
AND JULIAN SMITH

FOREWORD BY JOHN N. MACLEAN

wm
WILLIAM MORROW
An Imprint of HarperCollinsPublishers

HarperCollins books may be purchased for educational, business, or sales promotional use. For information please e-mail the Special Markets Department at SPsales@harper collins.com.

FIRST EDITION

Designed by Lisa Stokes
Maps of smokejumper bases and response times © by Jenn Tate

Library of Congress Cataloging-in-Publication Data has been applied for.

ISBN 978-0-06-231962-3

15 16 17 18 19   OV/RRD   10 9 8 7 6 5 4 3 2 1

I dedicate this book to my dad, for teaching me that a handshake and the word of a man is all he has, and without that, you're nothing

Fire has always been and, seemingly, will always remain, the most terrible of the elements.

HARRY HOUDINI

I've always followed my father's advice: he told me, first to always keep my word and, second, to never insult anybody unintentionally. If I insult you, you can be goddamn sure I intend to. And, third, he told me not to go around looking for trouble.

THEODORE ROOSEVELT

CONTENTS

NCSB

Missoula

Grangeville

Redmond

McCall

Boise

Redding

Smokejumper Bases *of the* American West

This map is a handpainted artist's rendering ana

Historical Bases
Cave Junction, OR
La Grande, OR
Idaho City, ID
Seeley Lake, MT
Nine Mile, MT
Wise, VA

Satellite/Spike Bases*
Galena, AK
Fairbanks, AK
McGrath, AK
Miles City, MT
Twin Falls, ID
Ogden, UT
Columbia, CA
Fresno, CA
Porterville, CA
Santa Maria, CA
Albuquerque, NM

West
owstone

N
NW NE
W   E
SW SE
S

Fairbanks

⭐ Silver City*

Satellite and/or spike bases vary from year to year depending on need. They can be set up and staffed nearly anywhere in the U.S. within 24 hours. This is just a partial list and does not include every one of these bases.

ed to be used for navigation or directions. Map copyright 2015 (+)

FOREWORD: OLD FIRES, NEW LIFE
by John N. Maclean

Over the past three-quarters of a century nearly six thousand men and women have served as smokejumpers, leaping from airplanes to fight fire in backcountry. It all started when fifteen firefighters died on the Blackwater Fire in 1937 in Wyoming backcountry. David Godwin, an assistant chief of the Forest Service and one of the fire investigators, concluded that the management of the fire was "intelligent and protective of the men." But it took so long to get to the fire that flames were far beyond control by the time firefighters arrived: a faster response by only a couple of hours, he concluded, might have saved fifteen lives.

Within two years, the smokejumper program was under development at Winthrop, Washington, and in Montana at Moose Creek and Seeley Lake. My family built a cabin on Seeley Lake in the early 1920s that we own and enjoy to this day; my father Norman Maclean, who was there when the early jumps were being made, later wrote about the smokejumpers first great tragedy, the Mann Gulch Fire of 1949, in his book,

Young Men and Fire: he went from the cabin to see the fire while it was still smoldering. I wrote about the next one in my book *Fire on the Mountain* (William Morrow, 1999), an account of the South Canyon Fire of 1994 in which three smokejumpers and eleven other firefighters died in the flames; I did a lot of the work at Seeley Lake.

Today, the smokejumper program is in trouble. Partly to blame is the loss of backcountry: development has encroached into previously wild country, a lot of roads have been built, and helicopters can land where there are no roads. Modern regulatory life being what it is, however, many fire supervisors are suspicious of the smokejumpers, always individualistic, sometimes arrogant, prone to jump injuries. Smokejumpers don't fit in well with the bureaucratic slowness that too often marks getting started on a fire. Supervisors often decline to call for smokejumpers as a first resort instead of taking advantage of their finer qualities: quick to a fire, capable of independent action, tireless, and an inspiration to others to perform at peak level.

The good news is that smokejumping's storied past may help maintain its future. Jason Ramos's *Smokejumper* is a rousing personal adventure story, a nutshell history of the great wildland fires, and an insider's brief for making smokejumpers more relevant on today's fire line. "Jumpers are the Swiss Army knives of wildland firefighting," Ramos writes. "We don't just parachute into remote fires. We can also make it to close-in fires by helo or vehicle, often faster than anyone else."

Ramos is a Puerto Rican kid from suburban Los Angeles, small as smokejumpers run, who put in years as a municipal firefighter and helitack, shunned minority preferences, hid a serious injury, and eventually achieved his ambition to become a smokejumper. That's enough material for a book, but there are other smokejumper books around—and probably more to come as more jumpers step out of parachute harness and take up the pen.

What distinguishes *Smokejumper* is Ramos's mixing of fire history and personal anecdote. He interspersed his own story with brief accounts of the great wildland fires of the past, from the catastrophic Upper Middle West fires of the nineteenth century to the Yarnell Hill Fire of 2013. Ramos has personal ties to several of these fires: he lost a friend and mentor on the 1994 South Canyon Fire and went to the Thirtymile Fire in 2001 while it still burned, after it took the lives of two teenage girls and two young men on a fire crew. History comes to life through Ramos's personal connections.

The sites where these fires happened are more than sacred ground, the stories of what happened there more than tales of misadventure, and the casualty lists more than footnotes to history—though they are all these things too. Old fires carry embers that can turn to flame and teach new lessons to later generations. Firefighters can walk where others like them walked, face the decisions they made, and try to imagine how they would have handled a life-threatening situation. Civilian visitors get a strong dose of the price mostly young people pay to defend forests and homes, and may come away determined to do their part to make their homes defensible. These days, as fire seasons start earlier and end later, as fires burn hotter and become less predictable—and those who fight them do not doubt that's what's happening—everyone needs a greater awareness of the stakes involved. The spirit of these sites is always there to be discovered, but you have to look for it. *Smokejumper* is an invitation to do just that.

I met Ramos while I was researching the Thirtymile Fire and he was the public information guy for the North Cascades Smokejumper base in Winthrop, a couple of dozen miles from the site of the fire. The base managers kindly extended barracks privileges to me on several occasions, and Ramos and I became friends. He was a bundle of energy then and is the same today, running his own gear company, writing a book, and still jumping fires. But he also has a conscience. Sadly, none of the lessons from the past have stopped wildland fire tragedies from happening again in the future. As Ramos notes, the Granite Mountain Hotshots took a detour from a fire assignment to visit Storm King Mountain, site of the South Canyon Fire, a few years before they met their own tragedy in 2013, and they vowed nothing like that would ever happen to them. You cannot change the basic nature of fire, which is fiercely unpredictable in the extreme. But you can try to keep alive the lessons of the past to give those of us who live with fire better odds, and this Ramos has helped to do.

THIS BOOK IS A memoir based on my recollection of past experiences over the years. I have done my best to fact-check
my memory against any and every factual record I could find,
as well as the memory of those who were there with me. When
records were not available, I re-created events, interactions, and
conversations, to the best of my ability. If I have misstated, mis-
interpreted, or misremembered anything, I apologize deeply
and sincerely in advance. No current jumpers' names are in this
book, out of deference to their privacy.

As soon as I entered the fire service, back as a seventeen-
year-old volunteer, I began to learn about the vast and mostly
unknown legacy of the brave pioneers who served long ago. I
hope this book is enjoyed by many and that it helps to inspire a
new generation to carry on this proud tradition—not only for
the smokejumper program, but for the entire fire service.

Sincerely,
Jason A. Ramos

PROLOGUE

"ARE YOU READY?"

The spotter* was shouting into the side of my helmet. His voice rose above the roar of the plane's engines and the wind howling through the open door.

My jump partner glanced out the door, then made way for me. I only had a moment to look out over the rippling green expanse of the Ochoco Mountains in central Oregon.

My left hand was on my red reserve chute handle, my right gripped the bar alongside the door of the plane. The rushing air rippled the heavy fabric of my jumpsuit. My pockets bulged with gear.

A few seconds after I left the plane, the static line that trailed over my left shoulder was supposed to open the parachute on my back automatically. If anything went wrong that I couldn't fix on exit, I could always pull the red handle of the reserve chute on my chest. From fifteen hundred feet, roughly

---

* A glossary of potentially unfamiliar terms appears on page 219.

halfway to the ground, I'd have twelve seconds to do this and still land safely. At fourteen seconds I'd become a permanent part of the scenery. At least that's what was drilled into our heads in training.

At twenty-six I already had years of experience fighting fire under my belt, including six seasons rappelling out of a helicopter in California. In five weeks of training as a rookie smokejumper I had already made nineteen successful jumps from a plane, on top of countless practice jumps from the Tower . . .

But like my four other rookie brothers on the plane, this would be the first time putting the two together. My first fire jump.

Was I ready?

Hell yeah. I was ready to go.

SAY THE WORD *SMOKEJUMPER* and the response—if people have heard of us at all—is usually something along the lines of: Aren't those the crazy guys who parachute into forest fires?

Well, no, not exactly. For starters, it wouldn't make much sense to land *in* fires if we possibly can help it, would it? We aim close, not in.

Second, we're not all guys; women have been jumping since 1981.

And, last, we're only partly crazy. Depends on how you define crazy, really. You'll probably find a slightly different answer if you ask a jumper. Smokejumpers are actually very highly trained and experienced wildland firefighters, not to mention extremely safety conscious.

After all, we've been doing this since the first silk canopies popped open over central Washington in 1939. We've had time to get it right, and our success rate—and safety record—reflect that.

So why all the misconceptions about a profession that's older than World War II?

One reason is there aren't that many of us. While the numbers vary each year, there are fewer than 500 jumpers on duty in the United States at any given time. Fewer than six thousand people have ever earned their smokejumper wings—total.

And jumpers on the whole are a modest bunch. Self-effacing, publicity shy, call it what you will, but tooting your own horn is definitely not part of the mentality. After fifteen years of being a smokejumper, I'm still amazed at how little people know about what we do. And more important, why.

Giving public tours of our base in Winthrop, Washington, I get that question all the time: How can you do this for a living? Why take two activities, parachuting and fighting wildfire, that in themselves would be too much for most people—and *combine* them?

How do you train for it? What does it do to your personal life? What's it like to have this as your full-time job? How do you not die? How do you have a spouse?

Answering those questions is part of the reason I wrote this book. I want to share what it's like to be a U.S. smokejumper, a job that's as rewarding as it is respected.

It's not a job everyone can do, not even close. But someone has to do it. And those who choose to—and all those who have in the past—have served our country with honor and bravery since 1939. The program deserves to have its story told.

I'm just one guy. There are jumpers who have done it longer, gotten hurt worse, and had closer calls or moments of heroism I could never hope to equal. I've included some of their stories here too.

In telling my own story, though, I want to show that appearances aren't everything. Even if someone is quiet, doesn't carry on or seek the spotlight—like almost every jumper I know—it doesn't mean he or she is arrogant or condescending.

When the mission's on, we're savages. But in the end we're just people, even if our job is a little different than most.

We don't do it for the glory or the glamour. We provide a meaningful public service, one that's part of a proud legacy.

This is what we do.

STANDING IN THE DOOR of the plane, the first, most important goal was reaching the ground in one piece.

On the flight in, we had all sat cocooned in our suits and helmets, alone with our thoughts. My mind was buzzing like the plane's propellers. I silently ran through all the different ways a parachute could malfunction, and what I needed to do in each case to stay alive.

Through the metal mesh of my face mask, I glanced toward the front of the plane. Those of us sitting further back could only see out to the sides. But the jumpers closest to the cockpit, those who would be last in the load to jump, could already see the header—the plume of smoke from the fire—miles out. They turned and faced the rear of the plane, and their hand gestures, body movements, and facial expressions told us clearly that this was no small fire. Down below, the lightning-sparked fire already covered ten or fifteen acres—as we call it, a "going fire." Definitely not a two-manner.

Like the rest of the others I looked out the window, watching the smoke and streamers, picking out a landmark to make sure I'd land facing into the wind as we had been trained.

We knew we were on station, over the fire, when the pitch of the engines fell. The pilot throttled back to drop speed and started orbiting left, the side the door was on. It was like taking a long, curving freeway off-ramp.

Things started to happen fast. Weighted crepe paper streamers fluttered to the ground, showing which way the wind blew and how long it would take us to touch down.

The spotter started issuing commands.

Jumpers began to leave the plane in pairs a few seconds apart.

When our turn was up, my jump partner and I stepped forward to the door, and listened for the spotter's commands.

"Leg straps tight?" I gave a thumbs-up.

"Hook up." I connected my static line and gave it a small tug. Now came a quick pre-jump briefing—short and sweet.

"Did you see the streamers and the jump spot?"

We nodded, shouted "Yes!"

"Stay the fuck out of the fire, rookie!"

Within seconds, the plane was turning on its final pass for our designated exit point. The spotter shouted the last commands.

"Turning final, fifteen hundred feet. Your static line is clear," to my partner. And then to me: "Your static line is clear."

"Get in the door." I stepped toward the open door, right behind my partner.

The spotter slapped him on the leg, the signal to jump. Out he went.

It was my turn. Everything I'd trained for the last five weeks came down to this: no hesitation, no second thoughts. Just muscle memory and the mission.

I launched out into the void.

CHAPTER 1

L ATE-SUMMER SUNRISE OVER THE Owens Valley, 1992. Snow lingers on the orange-lit Sierra Nevada to the west.

Across the wide basin, Telescope Peak and the rest of Death Valley is silhouetted in the morning glare.

A gray '72 Chevy LUV, packed with gear, rolls north up Route 395 along the base of the mountains.

At the wheel is a nineteen-year-old Puerto Rican kid from the SoCal suburbs, anxious and excited, on his way to start an ass-kicking new job in the middle of nowhere.

That's me.

A week earlier I had gotten an offer for a seasonal position in the California Desert District, working on an engine crew with the Bureau of Land Management (BLM). During the long, dark drive north, I had plenty of time to wonder what exactly I was getting into. Is the captain going to be a hard-ass? Can I handle the workload? Will the crew eat me alive?

Growing up in Los Angeles and Riverside Counties, I had already seen my share of crazy shit. From the natural disasters that plagued the state—earthquakes, floods, forest fires—to the drug-fueled violence of the 1980s, era of *Boulevard Nights* and *Colors*, California was not a boring place to live.

In a year with the Riverside County Fire Department, I'd rolled out to fatal house fires, cardiac arrests, and bloody car accidents. I had even worked several wildfires, though nothing too big. (I burned my foot on my very first one, walking through the flames like a greenhorn rookie.)

I had no plans after high school. College wasn't an option; my grades sucked. Law enforcement was out since, in my world, "cop" meant "narc." I thought about going into the military, hopefully as a long-range marksman. I grew up precision shooting with my dad. By the time I was in my late teens, my dad's challenge was for me to shoot the head of FDR out of a dime at a hundred yards—that part was easy—then to put four more shots behind it—a little bit more difficult. So a job that used those skills sounded interesting.

But something about fire had always fascinated me. Like every boy and half the girls in America, I played with toy fire engines and put out imaginary blazes when I was young.

I remember standing on the roof of our house in my early teens with my father, watching a wildfire eat up a hillside just a few blocks away. I had never seen anything like it: the incredible, almost industrial heat, the hum of activity, the sheer relentless power of the flames.

The air was filled with an eye-stinging haze, the blare of fire engines, and the buzz of helicopters. Fat air tankers swooped in to dump loads of rust-colored retardant.

It was mesmerizing, like staring into a campfire the size of a city. At one point I started to climb down off the roof. My father asked what the hell I was doing, told me to stay put.

I just wanted to see it up close.

My two older brothers and I did our fair share of backyard combustion: firecrackers, M-80s, gasoline, anything that would go boom. Hardly a day would go by without something blowing up or being charred to an unrecognizable mess.

My oldest brother worked as a U.S. Forest Service firefighter in the Angeles National Forest. In junior high I would sneak into his room and check out his gear, still scented like a campfire from days in the woods.

So when the BLM offer came, I jumped at the chance. Filling out paperwork at the local office, I heard a radio squawking in the background. A dispatcher was trying to contact an engine in the field. The call went out, over and over, with nothing but static in response.

Wow, I thought. *These guys are so far off the grid they're even out of radio range.*

This is going to be awesome.

The day before I had crammed my stuff into my pickup and rolled out of my parents' driveway at 3 A.M. My mother had packed me a cooler full of home-cooked Puerto Rican meals in Ziploc bags—chicken and rice (*arroz con pollo*), meat-stuffed potatoes (*rellenos de papa*), all the good stuff.

My parents, first-generation immigrants from San Juan by way of the Bronx, had taught me to always be punctual. As a firefighter I'd had it drummed in even deeper: always ready, never late. It's part of our motto.

This was my first time truly on my own. I couldn't wait to start.

The sun revealed the tiny town of Olancha, barely more than a few buildings and an intersection, at the south end of what was left of Owens Lake.

The story of how the lake was sucked almost dry to supply the booming city of Los Angeles was made famous in the movie *Chinatown*. Now the dry lake bed causes dust storms so bad they close down the highway.

I was an hour and a half early. I decided to take a slow recon past the fire station, which turned out to be more or less a mobile home. Parked next to it was a huge, bright yellow truck that looked like something Mad Max would buy if he won the lottery.

An older guy in a T-shirt and swim trunks was working on a Volkswagen bus nearby. Off to one side was a pile of windsurfing boards and gear.

At least that's one coworker I might get along with, I thought.

I ate breakfast in town and returned to the station. Inside was a small, clean office with mountain bikes leaning against one wall. A man came out of a hallway wearing a pair of underwear and nothing else.

"You the new guy?" I nodded and shook the hand of my new station manager.

"Sit tight, you're a little early," he said, and disappeared.

I knew this was normal—a firehouse is home to anyone on duty, with everything that implies—but I was tired from the long drive, and that initial eyeful gave the moment a touch of the surreal.

A few minutes later another dude emerged. He had clearly just woken up, but at least he had clothes on.

"Hey, Snapperhead," he said, quoting Andrew Dice Clay. "You're the new guy?"

From then on I was officially "Snapperhead," or just "Snapper." I hadn't been here half an hour and I already had a nickname.

It could have been a lot worse, I figured.

The other three crew members eventually wandered in, all rugged-looking guys my age or older. As everyone milled around getting ready for the day, I watched the Old Kahuna I'd seen outside put on a pair of logger-style boots with two-inch heels.

As a firefighter, I'd always been taught your boots were one of your most important pieces of equipment, and you should treat them accordingly. Take care of them, and they'll take care of you.

This guy laced his with such precision it was riveting.

A FEW MORNINGS AFTER I arrived, the station manager said, "Let's go for a run, Snapperhead." I followed him east, squinting into the rising sun.

This is it, I thought—*if I can't keep up with him, I'm done.*

I stuck to him like Velcro as we ran and ran. I kept up, but it hurt.

"You're in shape, at least," he muttered when we finished. "We'll go for a real run this week."

AS THE WEEKS PASSED, I gradually started to relax and feel truly a part of the six-man crew.

We were in the BLM's California Desert District, which covers about a quarter of the state, including parts of the Mojave and Sonoran Deserts.

In other words, one big tinderbox.

We responded to wildfires in remote rural areas and pretty much anything that came in through 911 except medical emergencies. Part of the job involved helping out the local volunteer fire department with structural fires and vehicle accidents, which I was more than familiar with from my time at Riverside.

Some missions lasted for days. One took us to Fort Hunter Liggett, an army fort south of Monterey, where soldiers practiced field maneuvers and trained with live ammo. At one point we drove out of a valley in the middle of nowhere and found ourselves face-to-face with two or three tanks and a dozen camo-clad soldiers fully decked out in gear and guns.

Times like that I was glad we were in the Mog, that crazy machine that stood guard beside the firehouse. Unimog, its full name, stands for UNIversal-MOtor-Gerät, or "universal motor machine," in German. These Mercedes-built monsters can do damn near anything: fight fires, plow snow, or carry heavy equipment, anywhere from the mountains to the desert to the jungle.

We could follow fire dozers into steep terrain, where I quickly learned why it had "oh-shit" handles all over the inside. Seeing other firefighters watch us drive through parts of the fire line was priceless. (Supporting ground troops was always equal parts "go-go-go" and "get-the-hell-out-of-here.")

Our Mog was bright BLM yellow, with red lights and sirens for clearing traffic. It had a front blade like a bulldozer, so we could plow our way into remote places other vehicles couldn't go.

On lunch breaks during fire operations, I would sit in the shade underneath the chassis. It took a full-sized Dodge Ram pickup with an extended bed just to carry the spare tire. When we came to a stop, the Mog would rock for a few seconds like a boat.

Can you tell I loved that engine?

When you work for the fire service, your job consists of waiting for something to go wrong and being ready to go the moment it does.

Even when we weren't out on a fire, the days were still full: PT, physical training, first thing in the morning, followed by checking and rechecking our gear, cleaning the station, keeping the Mog running smoothly.

The station is your home, so there's an endless list of maintenance duties to keep it livable, from pulling weeds to painting. Sometimes there was another PT session in the late afternoon.

In our off-hours we explored the area by car or on foot or mountain bikes. The stark landscape was straight out of a John Wayne movie—literally. Just about every western star in the business, including the Duke, filmed dozens of classics out here, from *True Grit* to *The Good, the Bad, and the Ugly*.

This was extreme country. Draw a line between the highest and lowest points in the Lower 48—the top of Mount Whitney and Badwater Basin in Death Valley, only eighty-five miles apart—and it goes almost exactly through Olancha.

I often wandered off into the Mojave alone, catching reptiles or just enjoying the solitude. The only drawback of the isolation was that the only good-looking females around had scales and claws. The desert was full of collared lizards, rattlesnakes, and desert iguanas, to name a few.

The Old Kahuna introduced me to some hot springs out on the southern end of Owens Lake. The mineral-rich water stank of sulfur—we called it "Dirty Socks"—but it was a relaxing spot to soak on cool desert nights, as long as you were prepared to spend the evening smelling a fair share of rotten eggs. It helped to breathe through your mouth.

I ended up getting along with him better than most of the others at the station. He would work for the BLM for six months and then take off for Baja California, Mexico to windsurf for the winter.

One evening we were at the springs with two other guys who went off four-wheeling in the dunes nearby. Everyone else was gone. When the Kahuna tried to start his VW, the engine wouldn't kick over.

Shit. I was hungry, thirsty, and tired, and now we were stranded. I knew firefighters loved to screw with the new guys. What did they have planned for me out here in the middle of nowhere?

"Hungry, Snapperhead?" came a shout.

Somehow the Kahuna had produced a full kitchen, complete with a well-stocked pantry, from the back of the van.

We ate cans of Spaghetti-Os under the stars. They were the best I ever had, buckaroo style. I was learning to always be ready—and to take life as it comes.

As a seasonal wildland firefighter, you're always aware you can be laid off at any time, or at least not rehired. It's often due to forces beyond your control: budget changes, good or bad fire years, and so on.

And the competition is tough: every winter thousands of applicants put in for seasonal positions for the coming year. So even as I settled in in Olancha, I kept my eyes open for other opportunities.

One possibility was to apply to become a hotshot. These highly trained and experienced crews attack wildfires throughout the United States, typically in teams of twenty to twenty-two. They're mostly employed by the Forest Service or the BLM (Bureau of Land Management), the BIA (Bureau of Indian Affairs), the National Park Service, and some state and county agencies. Highly skilled and motivated, hotshot crews typically live, eat, sleep, and train together six months of the year. Due to their experience and training, they're usually assigned to the more complex and rugged portions of fires and adapt to meet the needs of Incident Commanders in a variety of situations. They can build fire line, perform burnouts and backfires, fell trees, mop up after operations, build fences, or even assist organizations like FEMA with disaster assistance after hurricanes, tornadoes, and floods. Every hotshot takes great pride in not only being a hotshot, but also in upholding the high standards set before them from their founding members.

Hotshots are Type 1 crews. The term "Type 1" comes from the incident command system (ICS), used nationwide to coordinate emergency response. "Incidents" include everything from fire and other natural disasters to terrorist attacks and disease outbreaks. Responses are categorized based on size, from Type 5 (small) to Type 1 (very large).

Like anything official, ICS is a sea of acronyms. An incident commander (IC) usually directs an incident management team (IMT) out of an incident command post (ICP).

Just remember: Type 1 means biggest and baddest, whether you're talking about resources like aircraft and vehicles (Type 1 are the largest) or personnel—Type 1 teams like hotshots and smokejumpers typically have the most training and experience.

Hotshots work as hard or harder than anyone on a fire. Their main job is digging the fire line—clearing away anything flammable, down to mineral soil, to stop the fire's spread—and they're good at it. It's an ass-kicking job, with shifts of sixteen hours or longer followed by nights spent sleeping on the ground.

These guys are tough motherfuckers.

I didn't find any hotshot positions open at the time. Then my captain introduced me to a friend of his who was the assistant foreman on a Forest Service helitack crew.

These crews, as you can probably guess, use helicopters to reach remote fires. The idea is to arrive quickly, while the fire is still small, and get it under control before it grows. Sometimes helitack crews rappel to the ground. The BLM, BIA, National Park Service, and Forest Service all have helitack crews, as do some counties and cities.

I had never been on a helicopter. To be honest, I'm not too fond of heights. I love roller coasters and going fast. But even climbing tall ladders with my father, with a tool bag strapped around my shoulders, would always result in some serious puckerage until my feet touched the ground again.

Still, sliding down a rope from a helicopter to fight wildfires sounded like a challenge, an honor, and a privilege, something not many people have the chance to do. I wanted to serve, and I also wanted to be part of the best the fire service had to offer.

So I applied and was offered the position. When my three-month BLM season was over, I joined a Forest Service helitack crew in Kernville, at the southern end of the Sierras.

The crew had a reputation for tough PT, so I had spent the few months before I arrived getting in good shape.

Or so I thought.

KERNVILLE WAS A GOLD Rush town on the northern tip of Lake Isabella, a reservoir formed by the Kern River.

The river, fed by Sierra snowmelt, was busy with rafters, kayakers, and fishermen from spring through fall. Boaters and families played on the lake, and the steep forested mountains of the Sequoia National Forest rose in every direction.

It was a land of monsters. Some of the giant sequoias were over three hundred feet high and thirty-five hundred years old. And according to legend, this was Bigfoot country, too.

Another local giant was called Helitack Hill. Every base or fire station has a hill for training on, complete with nickname and a long history of pain. This was Kernville's.

I got my ass handed to me on the very first PT hike. We started with a gradual climb that turned into rocky stair steps climbing up and up and up, forever.

I was used to the rolling hills at home, not this mountain goat crap.

I kept my head down and vowed the only way I was stopping was if I choked on my own vomit, passed out, and rolled down the hill.

Somehow I made it to the end with the contents of my stomach still in place. But I never really got used to those training hikes. They could last up to two hours on a "special" day. Sometimes we had to hike the hill twice as punishment for some screwup.

One hike they called "Tablets," because on occasion new crew members had to carry a stone that looked like it could have been one of the Ten Commandments. As the story went, when you got to the top you would be speaking in tongues.

I witnessed this transformation more than once.

I learned quickly that on this crew, it didn't matter if you were sick or felt like crap—you still had a job to do. Otherwise you'd never hear the end of the shit.

Guys would throw up during a run or a workout and say "I'm good, let's go." Others would just run until they dropped, so they wouldn't get chewed out for stopping by choice.

Our supervisor's favorite bit of advice for quitters: "McDonald's is hiring, and I know they could use a good worker like yourself."

Don't get me wrong—this was an exciting time. I was almost twenty, moving on my own through the world of wildland firefighting.

I'd gone from wondering whether I'd see my eighteenth birthday to doing one of the coolest things I could have imagined.

EVERY MORNING WE ASSEMBLED at the heliport at zero nine hundred, ready for duty. It was best to be early. The supervisor hated lateness, and he loved to assign crappy chores or extra PT to slackers.

We stood at attention, hats in hands, as one of us raised the American flag. Other stations I'd worked at just had automatic lights that turned on and off at night to illuminate the flag. I wish every fire department took the time to show the respect of actually raising the colors.

Then it was time to check our gear, do load calculations, and outfit the helicopter. All our tools and equipment went into the cargo basket, along with a collapsible water bucket.

My first year we had a Bell 206 JetRanger. When you think "helicopter," this is probably the image that pops into your mind. It's the kind you see hovering above city highways reporting on traffic.

The one we had was a piece of junk, and it was too small to be a good firefighting platform.

My second year we became one of the few crews on our forest to use an Aérospatiale Alouette III 316B. That ship kicked serious ass. It could hold four firefighters plus a pilot. It looked like a dragonfly, with a big bubble of forward windows and a turbine nozzle above the tail like a rocket.

And man, was it loud. New guys were warned that a few seconds near the engine without ear protection could permanently damage their hearing. It couldn't even land at certain airports due to noise ordinances.

We trained for hours on end until we could lift off within minutes of a call coming in. Everything needed to run like clockwork. "Kind of right" isn't good enough when even a tiny mistake can be serious, even deadly. Something as minor as a broken bungee cord could cause a rotor strike, not good.

Everyone had to know his or her exact place in the high-decibel choreography. Our superintendent (supt) and captain timed us on tasks like deploying the water bucket. If we took too long or, God forbid, did anything wrong, we'd pay for it with more hours of bucket drills, often in triple-digit temperatures.

We flew to fires across Southern California, Nevada, Montana, New Mexico, and Arizona.

The first step when we arrived at a fire was to evaluate the situation from the air. How big was it, how fast was it moving, and in what direction? What was the terrain like, and what was the weather doing? Where would be a good place to set down?

If possible, the first choice was to land the helicopter and just get off and go fight the fire. But if the ship couldn't land safely, we would relocate to a safe landing area and then configure for rappel operations. When you rappel out of a helicopter, one end of the 250-foot rope is fastened securely inside the ship and the other hangs off to the ground. In between, it's wrapped around a stubby metal gadget called a SkyGenie that is clipped to your harness with a locking carabiner.

More wraps around the "bone," as we called the Genie, create more friction, meaning a slower slide. It's the same kind of system used by search-and-rescue teams and high-rise window washers.

In the typical rappel exit, you stand on a step on the outside of the ship, then lean back until your head is lower than your feet. In that position you slide smoothly down the rope. You control your speed by how fast you feed the rope through the bone, with your brake hand, usually your right.

Our rappel trainer Rich Tyler, a helitack foreman for the BLM, was known for his attention to safety. He once refused to let the governor of Colorado fly in his helicopter until he put on a protective flight suit.

Rich taught us a different, "dynamic" style of rappelling. Picture this: you're standing on the helicopter step with the rope hanging down below you. To get to the dangling-in-midair part of the descent, first you have to get the bone past the step. Otherwise it will catch and the weight and momentum will mash your nonbrake hand into the metal, usually followed by your face.

How do you keep this from happening? First you squat down on the step and pull your brake arm up as far as possible, to create slack in the rope below you.

Then you hop backward into the void.

If you did everything right, the slack lets the bone clear the obstacle, you catch yourself with your brake hand, and you finish the descent in peace and good health.

If you didn't, well, as we said, "feed it or eat it."

CHAPTER 2

THE COOL MORNINGS MADE the rappel rope stiff and hard to feed through the bone.

There was another problem. The protocol for all helitack rappelers was to use the same number of wraps on the bone—two—for everyone, regardless of their weight.

The motivation was supposedly for safety; a large person who didn't have enough wraps could take an unplanned express descent. But the single standard made it more challenging for people on the lighter end of the scale.

Like me.

On one particular morning I made my hop off the step fine. I didn't have enough slack, though, and the rope didn't feed through the bone fast enough.

With my full weight on the rope, the bone caught my left index finger against the step. It felt like someone had smacked my hand with a sledgehammer.

The pain didn't hit for a few seconds. By the time I worked the bone over the step, though, I could feel something warm and wet running down my forearm.

I figured I had just lost a finger.

This particular rappel involved doing an emergency tie-off, where you stop your descent so you get both hands free. I finished the procedure, although it took a little longer than usual.

By the time I reached the ground, a small pool of blood had gathered in the elbow of my fire shirt. I took my glove off. The finger looked like a split grape. Thankfully it was still connected.

At the hospital, the small-town doctors did the best they could to sew my fingertip back together. It never looked or felt quite right again. The next day I was back on duty with a gigantic white bandage and no idea how I was going to get my gloves on.

As far as I know, no helitack crew uses a dynamic-type rappel anymore.

RICH TYLER WAS A quiet, patient instructor, with a wife and a ten-month-old son. Just a few weeks after our training ended, he was dispatched to a fire on Storm King Mountain near Glenwood Springs, Colorado. He was eventually joined by four dozen other firefighters.

On the afternoon of July 6, 1994, my twenty-second birthday, the fire blew up. Half the people on the mountain ended up running uphill for their lives in a futile race against the flames. Rich and thirteen others never made it home.

I had been taught that death was a part of being a firefighter. I had attended a few funerals already.

Still, hearing what happened was a punch in the gut. It just didn't compute. How could this happen to someone who was so experienced and competent? As a firefighter you hear over and over how, if you do everything right and follow all the safety guidelines, you'll be fine.

It was sobering. No matter how competent and conscientious you are on a fire, sometimes bad shit just happens, even to the best of us.

My supervisor knew we all liked Rich. The next day on my way to the office, I was checking the cactus garden (part of our daily chores was to make sure the cactus garden was spotless), and he saw me and asked if I was okay.

"Yeah, I'm good," I said.

THE JOB DIDN'T OFFER time off to grieve. I had to process all this even as I practiced the skills Rich himself had taught me.

Rappelling to the ground was only the first step. As soon as we touched down and took off our rappel gear, we got busy cutting a fire line.

Fire doesn't just burn out in the open; it can hide under the surface in forest duff and other organic material. Embers can smolder for hours, even days, then burst back to life.

Exposing naked mineral soil is the only way to control or stop a fire from spreading on the ground. (Through the air is another story.) Depending on the terrain and fuel type, a fire line can be anywhere from a foot or two wide to ten feet or more.

At the head of the line, teams of sawyers clear away anything flammable with chain saws. Swampers stand by to pull the cut material out of the way so the sawyers can concentrate on cutting.

Then come the diggers with hand tools, scraping and digging.

Over the years, wildland firefighters have developed an arsenal of specialized tools for grubbing line in different conditions.

A few you'd recognize, like shovels and axes. Some are vaguely familiar, like the hoe on steroids called a rhino.

Others look like the bastard offspring of two or three tools, combined for brutal efficiency. A McLeod is a sharp hoe backed by a sturdy rake. A pulaski, probably the most iconic wildfire tool, is an ax with a thick horizontal blade on its back side.

Any of our firefighting tools would make a Viking marauder proud.

There's a constant influx of new tools as companies try to come up with new and innovative ideas, but they're often more flash than function. (I've found the ones that really work are designed by actual Type 1 firefighters.) The old standbys have earned that status for a reason.

I had no idea how proficient I'd eventually become with a pulaski. You can use it left- or right-handed to chop branches, dig holes, or scrape sod. With a little practice it throws pretty well, too, although that technique isn't covered in standard training. For digging line or fighting off an enraged Sasquatch, I'd reach for a pulaski.

To get a feel for cutting line, imagine a combination of logging and ditch-digging, in a steep hillside forest, under the California sun. You're wearing heavy leather boots and gloves and a hard plastic helmet. Your pants and long-sleeved shirt are made out of Nomex, a synthetic fabric designed for flame resistance (at the time not the best in breathability or comfort).

Then add the heat and smoke of a forest fire practically licking at your elbow.

Easy? No. Boring? Definitely not.

Rewarding? Hell yeah.

You can't beat the feeling of working your ass off in the face of everything Mother Nature feels like throwing at you.

Whether you accomplished your goals or just made some small progress toward them, the fact that you're still breathing, hopefully not freezing your balls off, and have some food in your stomach means you had a normal day in our book. And normal is good.

As our crew worked the fire, the helicopter could fetch water in the Bambi Bucket, a bright orange collapsible container that hung from a longline under the ship. Skilled pilots can scoop water right out of a river, lake, reservoir, beaver pond—heck, a swimming pool if they have to—and dump it on a fire with pinpoint accuracy.

If you were working under a high tree canopy that limited the pilot's visibility, you might have to help tender the bucket in by hand from the ground until it was exactly where it needed to be.

Helicopters can also start controlled burns—fires lit deliberately to reduce fuels—with a helitorch, which is basically a flamethrower dangling under the ship, controlled by the pilot using an electric switch.

At the helibase we had to mix the helitorch fuel with a thickening agent, alumagel, stirring up fifty-five-gallon batches with hand paddles. It was like making napalm ice cream in a barrel, while wearing a respirator, amid all the heat and noise of a helicopter base.

Not the best job, especially when the mixmaster stuck his hand in and said you had the mix wrong and had to start over.

As soon as the pilot took off with one barrel we were already working on the next one.

Another way to light fires on purpose was to use "ping-pong balls," which are great for burning off ground fuels without doing too much damage to the overstory.

These small plastic spheres are filled with potassium permanganate and then injected with a squirt of ethylene glycol, creating a little chemical firebomb with a twenty- or thirty-second delay.

They're shot out of a dispenser attached to the ship. It's like a paintball gun for pyromaniacs.

WHEN WE FINISHED A mission on the ground the helicopter would come pick us up, although we often had to spend the night out first.

In those days Kernville was known as a tough, well-respected crew. Our supervisor didn't cut us any slack. We didn't carry luxuries like tents for overnights. On cold nights the only heat came from the fire itself.

Sometimes we'd sleep on slopes so steep we had to dig a trench just to keep from rolling down the hill. I learned to bury coals or rocks heated in the fire to make a warm patch of dirt to lie on. If I got the dirt-to-coal ratio right, everything was good. If I wasn't careful, I'd end up burning my ass.

On multiday assignments we might be based out of a fire camp for up to a few weeks with dozens or hundreds or even thousands of firefighters. Some camps had mess halls, medical tents—and if you got lucky, showers and a phone.

A bad fire season in California could keep us busy for months. When it was really going off, we might get multiple missions in one day. Even when the skies were clear everywhere else, thunder cells would build over the Kern River and dump lightning into the dry vegetation. We'd dig line in the heavy brush and trees, with flaming pinecones rolling down all around us, starting more spot fires.

Flying in a helicopter is never dull—especially when you're roaring a few hundred feet over a glowing line of flames crawling across a hillside, leaving nothing but charred land and smoke in its wake.

Turbulence is normal when you're flying low through unstable air. Thunderstorms, fires, and mountain topography create strong and unpredictable winds. But sometimes it goes well beyond that.

Once on the way back to base, we hit a downdraft over Walker Basin, a windy valley south of Lake Isabella. I was sitting in the back, behind the superintendent. Suddenly all I could see through the windshield was ground. Everything in the ship floated up, weightless, our bodies straining against the seat belts.

Huh, I thought. *I guess this is it.* It's strange how your mind works in moments like that. Everyone was calm, including the pilot. He pulled out of the sudden dive with hardly a grunt of surprise.

The feeling of sudden, abrupt weightlessness eventually became just another part of the job.

Another time we were flying into a fire on the Tule Indian Reservation, twenty-five miles northwest of Kernville, when I looked out the window and saw a cloud of dust and flying extra debris.

"Emergency traffic, 522 is down, emergency traffic," squawked the radio. The voice betrayed no emotion, but we knew the order to clear the airwaves of everything but emergency communications meant something bad had happened.

Helicopter 522, another Alouette, had just crashed. Everyone knew the pilot, a vet whose combat experience in Vietnam made him fun to fly with. As we raced to help, everyone was wondering the same thing: Was there anyone else on board?

It looked like a longline had swung up and hit his tail rotor during bucket operations. That meant the pilot was alone at the controls.

By some miracle he survived.

IN BETWEEN SEASONS AT Kernville, I came home to volunteer with the Riverside County Fire Department and to help train new recruits.

One of my hairiest brushes with danger to that point in my career happened when I was back home. On a fire at Lake Perris State Park, just east of Riverside, I was assigned to a state engine that had room for one more. I didn't know any of the crew on board.

I was sitting in the open rear of the cab with another firefighter. As we drove along slowly, flames crawled closer and the temperature rose—so far, more or less a normal day on the job.

Then the fire gradually surrounded the engine. When I saw the other crew member grab the engine protection line, a short hose used to protect the engine itself, I knew things were starting to get interesting.

Like all fire engines with a rear open cab, we were equipped with fire curtains, heat-resistant barriers you can close to protect yourself from radiant heat and high temperatures. In an engine, this is the last tool you have to keep the heat off you, like your shower curtain keeps water off the bathroom floor.

I was thinking about grabbing the curtains when the engineer finally drove us out of there.

This seemed pretty hairy to me at the time. I was a seasoned rookie firefighter with nearly seven years of fighting fire under my belt. As the years went on, though, an episode like this would become not even worth mentioning at the end of the day. Just another part of the job.

ON A SEPTEMBER AFTERNOON my fourth season at Kernville, a small plane went down in Walker Basin and started a brush fire. There was at least one survivor, who had managed to make it out and call for help.

Everything seemed to conspire against us getting there on time. First we had to battle the local afternoon headwind flying down the canyon. Then, even though we had the Bambi Bucket hooked up in record time, a problem with the cable cost us valuable seconds.

I could see the smoke a few miles out and felt a maddening helplessness that we couldn't go any faster. It's terrible knowing there might be people trapped and you can't do anything until you get there.

We finally arrived at the crash site, on a sloping hillside covered in chaparral, dry grass, and a few scattered trees. The plane was a single-engine Piper 28 that had crashed during a flying lesson. One of the four people on board had been thrown out of the plane. He had tried to pull his companions, two men and a woman, to safety, but the wreckage exploded in flames before he could. Badly burned, he had made it to the nearest road and flagged down a car.

The wreckage was still smoldering. A crew of Forest Service firefighters was already on scene. It was clearly too late to help anyone.

Up close I could see odd, ragged scratches on the body of the plane, just outside one of the broken windows. It took a second before it hit me what they were.

One of the trapped passengers had survived the impact and tried to claw his or her way out.

A familiar odor lingered in the air.

"What the hell is that smell?" one of the local firefighters said, half joking.

I had to fight the urge to not walk over there and smack the helmet off his head for his lack of respect for the victims. He was obviously just a rookie and didn't know better.

I did. When I was eighteen, I was on a Riverside call to a residence just down the street from my house. Another volunteer was already there and together we went inside. The house was filled with smoke and a distinct smell I couldn't place. Not burning plastic or wood—more like cooked meat.

We found a woman inside, hysterical and deep in shock but unhurt. It took a few minutes to piece together what had happened.

The woman had told her husband she was leaving him. He went out to the garage and doused himself with gasoline. Then he lit himself on fire, walked into the house, and collapsed in the living room in front of her.

A trail of charred pieces marked his final route.

Standing on the hillside next to the smoldering fuselage, I recognized that smell.

There was no way we could have helped the people in the plane. I still felt like I had somehow failed them, though. It made me furious to think that they had survived the crash only to die in the flames, a far worse way to go.

That night back in Kernville I jerked awake in the darkness to find myself standing, drenched in sweat. I had no idea where I was or how I got there.

I looked around in a daze. Kitchen on the left, living room on the right. This was still the house I was living in at the time. I was down the hallway from the bedroom and it was the middle of the night. Through the windows, the faint lights of other homes flickered down on the valley floor.

I couldn't move. A deep, cold darkness like I'd never known seemed to freeze me from the inside out.

Slowly, feeling and movement seeped back into my body. I went back to bed and lay wide awake in the darkness for a bit wondering what the fuck just happened.

"You okay?" my girlfriend at the time said.

"Yeah, I'm okay." I took a long drink from the jug of cold water she always put by the bed for me.

Everyone deals with shitty missions differently. Some people shrug them off. Some can't handle it and quit. For others, including me, a gradual numbness seemed to build up.

You found yourself focusing on the technical details, the immediate parts you can actually control, as a way of insulating yourself against the emotional impact of the terrible things we saw almost every day.

Then out of nowhere it could hit you like a sack of wet potatoes, as my dad would say. A complete mental and emotional overload. For a few seconds it seemed like time stopped. But it would always start up again.

I must have fallen back asleep, because the next thing I knew it was morning.

Time to get up and go to work.

CHAPTER 3

I WORKED EIGHT SEASONS on the helitack crew. We were a tight bunch, upholding the Kernville reputation with pride.

When we weren't working or training, we still spent a lot of time together, playing sand volleyball and swimming in the lake. On high-water years you could swim right off the transit airport ramp.

After years of working with the same crew, I could recognize someone from a sneeze or fart in the dark or a silhouette digging line.

Eventually I moved up to lead crew member. Once for a few months, I filled in as captain for a short time, a position of greater responsibility and independence.

I started working more fires as incident commander. The higher IC rating you get, the more responsibilities you have.

Yet the longer I worked as a wildland firefighter, the more I heard about another, even more exclusive group: smoke-jumpers.

The first time I heard the term, in a National Geographic

documentary, I was in my teens. This was the late 1980s, the *A-Team* and *Rambo* years, and everything about them fit that mold: the small group, the intense training, the lethal dangers they faced daily.

As I moved through the ranks of the firefighting world, I picked up more info, all of it secondhand at first. Jumpers had the mystique of the elite, for better and worse. They were known for being highly trained, crazy fit, self-reliant, and egotistic.

You heard them called "arrogant bastards" a lot.

That was the stereotype, at least. The same people who called the hotshots the marines of wildland firefighting and likened helitack crews to the air force sometimes compared smokejumpers to special operations forces.

Firefighting and the military are two completely different worlds, of course. Smokejumpers were the cream of the crop, though. They were usually the most experienced and skilled firefighters on the scene. It was hard to find anyone who challenged that.

I eventually learned the roots of the stereotype firsthand: part jealousy, part resentment, and part truth. Being a jumper takes a certain kind of personality. You have to be independent and tough, both physically and mentally. To do the job, it's not enough to just survive. You have to be able to thrive in an environment that can kill you six ways before breakfast.

At Kernville all I knew was that smokejumpers were fascinating. Then I started crossing paths with them on fires around the West. They were rare, almost like a different breed. There were only fewer than 500 on duty any given season, and they tended to keep to themselves. Jumpers were usually older than your average hotshot or helitack crew member, at least in their late twenties if not thirties or forties, sometime even their fifties.

Having a jumper on a fire was a little like having a rock star in a restaurant: you couldn't help but be curious what all the fuss was about. Some people actually wanted to become smoke-jumpers, but even more just wanted to interact with them.

On a fire in Winnemucca, Nevada, I walked over to a BLM jumper who was busy stuffing gear into a bag.

"What's up?" I said. He just nodded curtly and kept pack-ing. *What a dickhead*, I thought. But damn, his gear was more exotic looking than anything we had. And his food looked much better than our shitty old MREs.

That night I was walking through town when I looked through the window of a bar and saw the same guy inside. There was something different about the way he held himself, standing alone with his drink like some old-time gunslinger. Regardless of the brush-off earlier that day, I saw confidence, not arrogance.

Whatever it meant, smokejumpers had an aura that was impossible to ignore. I wanted a piece of that.

Who wouldn't?

AROUND THAT TIME, WE were on a fire in the Sequoia National Forest near the Kernville helibase. The blaze had spread to a few acres, and it looked like we were going to need some help to put it out.

I overheard a radio call from our forest's fuels management officer (FMO), asking our superintendent's thoughts on having a load of jumpers brought in. Finally I'd get a chance to work with these guys.

"We don't need any," my supt said curtly. "We can handle it."

The radio was silent for a few seconds.

"Not negotiable," the FMO replied. He was a former jumper out of Missoula and he knew what they could do. "You will be getting a load of jumpers at this time. Do you copy?"

My supt looked like he had bitten on a bad tooth. Orders were orders, however.

A few hours later we heard the faint sound of a fixed-wing plane approaching. We watched as the jump ship circled over the fire. Someone tossed out long paper streamers that fluttered to the ground, showing which way the wind was blowing.

I was so stoked I could hardly stand still. There were huge boulders and hundred-foot trees everywhere, and the wind was starting to pick up. Where the hell were they going to land?

Parachutes blossomed in pairs overhead. The first two jumpers set down near us. They must have radioed back that it wasn't a good landing spot, because the rest landed in a meadow below us. Every touchdown was perfect.

As soon as they joined us on the fire, the jumpers immediately took charge and got to work. Their exertion left me speechless. I had never seen anyone dig in on a fire like that, hotshots or helitack. It looked like that load of eight jumpers could handle anything.

My helitack supervisor knew I was interested in smoke-jumpers. To his credit, he must have said something to someone, because the jumper in charge (JIC) found me as we were mopping up.

"So I hear you're interested in the program," he said.

"Yes, sir."

"Well, what can you offer us, Mr. Ramos?" I felt like a deer in the headlights. Was this a trick question? I'd been fighting fires since I was seventeen, and I had an unusually wide range of experience: Unimog, helitack, engines at Riverside. Not many people my age could say they've ridden a fire engine tailboard and rappelled out of an Alouette.

But all that vanished from my head in front of the JIC. He asked about my education and any other skills I had outside of fighting fire.

"I like boxing," I blurted. The second the words left my mouth I felt like a fool. Fighting? That's my talent?

"You might need it," he said and walked away.

The brief exchange showed me that becoming a smoke-jumper wasn't a crazy fantasy. It was something that could actually happen—if I could make the cut.

First I would have to get in the best shape of my life. Jumpers didn't just have to leap out of planes, climb into and out of giant trees, and dig line in the middle of nowhere. They also have to pack out everything they bring in with them.

Every ounce. On foot.

One day at the base I asked our FMO, the former Missoula jumper, for advice. He nodded toward Helitack Hill, which had already almost killed me more than once.

"When you're able to do that carrying 110 pounds," he said, "that should get you close for rookie training."

Close? For a second I thought he was kidding. I was five foot six and only weighed a little over 125 pounds soaking wet. But I quickly realized he was dead serious.

The first time I tried to heft a pack that heavy, I was in the exercise room at my parents' house. I loaded it with sandbags and square plastic water containers called cubies, which we used for drinking water on a fire. Each cubie held five gallons, a little over 40 pounds. I crammed in anything else I could to bring the total weight to just over 110 pounds.

I sat down on the floor, put my arms in the shoulder straps and tried to stand up. Instead I slowly tilted to one side, pack and all.

My father poked his head in the door and found me sideways on the floor, legs flailing like a drunk turtle.

"Need some help, son?" he said with a grin.

It took a few tries to figure out how to put on a pack that weighed almost as much as I did. You put it on sitting down—that part I got right—but then you have to maneuver onto your hands and knees. From there you can stand up, slowly and carefully. If there's a log or a rock or something to give you a little extra leverage, all the better.

Like a lot of smokejumper training, nobody tells you this; you have to work it out for yourself.

(Another thing you learn through experience: take very good care of the straps on your pack-out bags. If you blow out one of those in the middle of nowhere, you're screwed.)

I began training with the giant pack almost every day, alone and with friends. I started with quarter-mile hikes through the grapefruit groves near my parents' house in Lake Elsinore. Then half a mile, a mile, two. Then hills.

Back at Kernville my superintendent gave me extra time for training. I'm still not sure whether he was humoring me or setting me up to fail. Either way I could eventually make it up and down Helitack Hill with a fully loaded pack without crippling myself.

My knees can still feel it.

FOR THREE YEARS I trained like a madman and applied for every smokejumper rookie class I could. Rumors started to float around: *Ramos will never make it. He's overtraining. He's too old.* (I was twenty-five, near the rumored cutoff age for rookie smokejumpers, although in truth rookies have been hired into their fifties.)

I kept at it. Early one morning in the spring of 1999, during one of my return stints at Riverside, my mother knocked on my bedroom door. A smokejumper was on the phone.

Dammit, I thought. *Another "interest call" that won't go anywhere.* I'd already done this a dozen times. It was late in the hiring season, and I assumed I'd already missed the year's selection anyway.

I picked up the phone. It was Mr. Button, training foreman for the North Cascades Smokejumper Base (NCSB) in Winthrop, Washington, the birthplace of smokejumping.

He asked a number of questions I had answered before. Did I really think I was ready for the job? Was I in good shape?

"Tell me again your firefighting experience," he said.

"Going on ten years, sir."

"Ten seasons?"

"No sir, ten years. I work summers with the Forest Service and winters here in Riverside County."

"Well, why haven't you gotten hired yet?" It sounded like he was joking.

"I guess they don't like R-5 folks too much," I said. The Forest Service's Region 5 covered all of California, where overhead were notorious sticklers for regulations, and the fire conditions were among the most extreme in the country. So people tended to assume you were on the tight-assed, arrogant end of the spectrum.

I kept glancing at the clock as we chatted. I had an appointment in half an hour.

"Excuse me, sir," I said finally. "I don't mean to be rude, but I have to get going."

"Well, do you want this job or not?" he said.

"What?" I must have misheard him.

"I'm calling to offer you a job, Mr. Ramos."

My heart skipped a beat. I had wanted this so badly, for so long, that for a second I was speechless.

"What? Y-yes. Yes, sir!"

Later that morning I went out for my normal training run humming with energy. Rookie training started in June, just a few months away. I wanted to be able to run a sub-six-minute mile in hilly terrain by the time I reported.

I pushed it extra hard, and I kept pushing myself as the days went on. Over the next few weeks a dull ache took hold in my left leg. I ignored it at first—I hate going to the doctor—

but my brother finally convinced me to make an appointment.

In the doctor's office, my stomach clenched as an X-ray tech hung a ghostly image of my leg on the light board. He pointed to a faint line running down my tibia: a nice, clean hairline fracture.

Maybe I wasn't going to be joining the smokejumpers' historic ranks after all.

CHAPTER 4

RANGER ED PULASKI STOOD at the mouth of the mine tunnel, choking on smoke. He threw hatfuls of water on the blanket that covered the opening. When the support timbers started to smolder, he doused them too.

His men lay on the muddy tunnel floor, writhing and moaning in the sweltering darkness. One man stood up and made a desperate rush for the entrance.

Pulaski barred the way and drew his pistol.

"The first man who tries to leave this tunnel I will shoot," he said.

It was August 20, 1910, in the Coeur d'Alene National Forest near Wallace, Idaho, and outside the world was burning.

Ever since humans tamed fire, it has been our best friend and worst enemy. We first used it to cook and stay warm, to light up the night and scare off predators. In North America, native tribes set fires to improve grazing for game, to clear farmland, and to make war. When European settlers arrived, the endless forests and open prairies they found were in large part the result of repeated burns set by Native Americans.

Early urban fires were frequent and devastating; the Great London Fire of 1666 destroyed more than 80 percent of the city. In 1736, Ben Franklin founded America's first volunteer fire company in Philadelphia. Members of these "mutual fire societies" helped douse blazes on one another's properties, using leather buckets and early water-pumping engines.

The rise of concrete, steel, and iron construction lowered the risk of citywide fires during the eighteenth and nineteenth centuries. City governments started installing fire hydrants attached to public water mains and setting up their own professional fire departments. Cincinnati's was the first in the United States in 1853.

These men didn't just fight fires. They also fought each other over territory and the insurance money that came with putting out blazes. (Fire departments in New York City were notorious for sending out "runners" to get to fires first.) Some of the groups enlisted together to fight in the Civil War, which may be where the fire department rank system—company, battalion, captain, and so on—came from.

In the countryside, fire was a normal part of life well into the nineteenth century. Farming, logging, and railroad construction left the landscape littered with piles of slash and sawdust. Burning was the easiest way to get rid of them, and countless small man-made fires filled the skies with a hazy tang.

And of course, nature lent a hand.

In 1910, a dry spring in the northern Rockies was followed by an even worse summer. The first small lightning fires were already spotting the hillsides by June. Record summer temperatures baked the forests like pottery in a kiln.

Residents reported a feeling of impending doom in the

air. By August, thousands of small fires had sprung up across Washington, Idaho, Montana, and British Columbia, caused by everything from lightning to hobo campfires and sparking locomotives. Trains were such a problem that forest rangers had special rail-mounted bikes they pedaled down the tracks to snuff out the fires they left behind.

The U.S. Forest Service, founded as part of the Department of Agriculture only five years before, recruited an army of ten thousand men to help keep the blazes under control. Mostly immigrants, plus some soldiers and convicts, they were given shovels but no formal firefighting training.

On August 20, a freak cold front out of Washington State sent 75 mph winds through the mountains. The canyons acted like chimneys, sweeping all the small fires into the air and melding them into one giant inferno.

In two days, the "Big Burn" spread across western Montana, northern Idaho, and northeastern Washington. Telegraph operators described flame fronts thirty miles wide before the lines burned through. There was so much smoke that bats came out in the daytime and sailors hundreds of miles out in the Pacific couldn't see the stars.

There was no way to fight a fire this size. People were crushed by falling trees and baked alive in cellars. Firefighters shot themselves when their fire lines were overrun, dying mixed in heaps with horses and wildlife.

In places at the center of the blaze, like Wallace, Idaho, finding space on the last train out of town could mean the difference between living and dying. Soldiers had to order men off at gunpoint to make room for women and children. Even then they weren't safe. Engineers found the trestles over valleys were already on fire. They tried to hide in tunnels in the Bitterroot Mountains, but the oxygen-hungry flames still found them.

All people could do was run. An assistant ranger named Ed Pulaski rounded up forty-five firefighters near Wallace and tried to guide them to safety. Fire surrounded the group on the West Fork of Placer Creek in the Coeur d'Alene National Forest.

Pulaski had worked as a miner and knew about an old mine tunnel nearby with a seep running through it. He urged the men in that direction. They fled through the deafening roar of hill-sized flames and thousands of massive trees snapping like twigs in the giant updrafts and crashing downhill. One survivor likened it to "a thousand trains rushing over a thousand steel trestles."

A falling tree crushed one man. At one point a black bear fled alongside them. It felt like the world was ending.

They made it to the tunnel just as the flames swept over their trail. Pulaski ordered everyone to get inside and lie facedown. He hung a blanket across the opening and tried to keep it wet against the impossible heat.

Some men cried like children and others prayed for divine mercy. Only one tried to bolt.

Eventually everyone passed out.

A second cold front—this time with rain—finally extinguished the firestorm.

"The completeness of the destruction is indescribable," wrote a journalist from the Idaho panhandle. "Not a living thing can be seen for a distance of 20 miles." The fire even killed the fish in the streams, left them floating by the thousands.

Three million acres had burned, an area the size of Connecticut. Entire towns had been vaporized. At least eighty-five people died, most of them firefighters.

In the Placer Creek mine shaft, Pulaski somehow managed to keep the flames out and his men in. At 5 A.M. the next morning, forty men crawled from the tunnel black with soot, their clothes in rags. The other five would never wake up.

"Come outside, boys," one man said. "The boss is dead."

"Like hell he is," Pulaski said, pulling himself to his feet. He was blinded and burned, his lungs seared from the heat, but alive. It was two months until he could see again. He lived the rest of his life in Wallace, where his wife and adopted daughter had survived the fires.

Even if not for his heroics, "Big Ed" would still be remembered for the tool he invented later in life. A pulaski is still standard issue for wildland firefighters.

The Big Burn changed America's attitude toward forest fires dramatically.

There was already a strong antifire sentiment in the Department of Agriculture. Bernhard Fernow, who ran the USDA's forestry division from 1886 to 1898, blamed wildfires on "bad habits and loose morals." Gifford Pinchot, the first chief of the Forest Service, said they "encourage a spirit of lawlessness."

After 1910, fire became the enemy, to be fought by an army called the U.S. Forest Service. Congress poured money into the agency's fire-suppression efforts—even today, more than half its budget goes toward fighting fires—just in time for a run of large fires in the 1930s.

The Tillamook Burn, a series of four enormous fires

between 1931 and 1951, destroyed over five hundred square miles of Oregon's coastal forests. In 1933, in the midst of the Great Depression, a wildfire in Griffith Park in Los Angeles killed twenty-nine men from a road crew, called on—and in some cases forced—to fight the fire for forty cents an hour.

The new head of the Forest Service, a survivor of the Big Burn named Gus Silcox, decreed that all forest fires should be controlled by 10 A.M. the day after they started. The problem was that wildfires usually started in such remote areas that they grew large before anyone could get in to fight them.

In August 1937, a lightning strike in Wyoming's Shoshone National Forest sparked a fire that went undetected for two days. By the time crews arrived, it had grown from two acres to two hundred. The Blackwater Fire eventually exploded into a firestorm that killed fifteen firefighters and injured thirty-eight more.

There had to be a better way to get men on a small fire, no matter how remote it was, without making them slog for miles over mountain trails carrying heavy equipment.

Although fixed-wing airplanes and modern parachutes were both barely more than thirty years old, World War I had spurred quick development in both. In the 1920s and 1930s, American foresters experimented with dropping water and chemicals on fires from airplanes, using everything from paper bags to beer kegs.

The idea of parachuting men in to fight forest fires originally came in 1934 from T. V. Pearson, an intermountain regional forester in Ogden, Utah. A professional parachutist even made a successful demonstration jump. Still, the higher-ups weren't convinced. This was the barnstorming era, and anything related to airplanes—let alone jumping out of them—was considered crackpot at best.

One memo said the Forest Service had "no hankering to assume the responsibility for men risking their lives in any such undertaking," since "all parachute jumpers are more or less crazy."

That didn't discourage David P. Godwin, the assistant chief of USFS Division of Fire Control, who was heading up the Forest Service's Aerial Fire Control Experimental Project. When the aerial bombing experiments didn't work, Godwin decided to use the leftover funding to try firefighting by parachute. The project was moved to a small dirt airstrip outside of Winthrop, Washington, in 1939.

The tiny lumber town in the Methow Valley of the North Cascades already had been a center for training fire personnel and had a variety of extremely rugged terrain nearby for testing. If parachute firefighting could work here, the thinking went, it could work anywhere.

That October, a team of sixteen foresters and parachutists started experimenting with parachutes. The first drops from the plane used 150-pound test dummies strapped to thirty-foot silk canopies made by the Eagle Parachute Company of Lancaster, Pennsylvania. They used the first USFS aircraft, a Stinson SR-10 Reliant, for the experimental jumps.

Then it was time for the volunteers. Seven of the eleven jumpers had never jumped before. A few had never even been up in a plane.

The jumpers wore two-piece padded canvas suits and

leather football helmets fitted with wire face masks to guard them from sharp tree branches. Wide leather belts and athletic supporters protected their spines and soft parts, respectively. They laced leather ankle braces over stout logger boots, and each man wore a twenty-seven-foot backup chute in a chest pack and carried a rope for rappelling out of trees.

The team included the Derry brothers—Frank, Chet, and Virgil—and Francis Lufkin, a fire guard with the Forest Service who had originally been hired to help the parachutists get down out of trees. The other jumpers started razzing Lufkin—how could he climb a tree but not jump out of a plane? He took it as a dare, one thing led to another, and soon he was suited up to jump too.

In six weeks in October and November, the crew made fifty-eight successful jumps into the Chelan (now Okanogan) National Forest, including the first jumps into timber. They jumped from two thousand to six thousand feet and landed in open meadows and on steep slopes littered with boulders.

When they pulled their rip cords, the chutes opened with a bang that could be heard five miles away. But there were only minor injuries—a twisted knee, a branch-scraped face—and every jumper walked away from the landing ready to fight a fire.

The next step was to find one. For the 1940 fire season, thirteen jumpers from Winthrop and Seeley Lake, Montana, were stationed at Moose Creek, Idaho. They all had to be men with wildland firefighting experience, between twenty-one and twenty-five years old. They received ten days of classroom and physical training and a salary of $193 per month, with no overtime or hazard pay. Johnson's Flying Service, a private contractor based in Missoula, supplied the planes and pilots.

On July 12, 1940, just thirty-seven years after the Wright Brothers invented the airplane, Earl Cooley and Rufus Robinson made the first fire jump in U.S. history.

It was a small lightning fire in the Nez Perce National Forest. The winds were so high they probably shouldn't have jumped. Cooley's chute came out of his pack tangled. It barely opened in time to deposit him in a spruce tree, ninety feet up.

Then the spotter almost fell out when the plane hit an air pocket.

Nevertheless, Cooley and Robinson made it to the ground safely and had the fire under control by the following morning. The next fire jump came two weeks later, and then Francis Lufkin and Glenn Smith made the first fire jumps in Winthrop that August. By the end of the season, smokejumpers had put out nine fires in Washington, Idaho, and Montana, saving an estimated $30,000.

Since the program's entire budget was $9,047, that qualified it as a major success.

Two jump bases were in operation by the end of 1940. One was at the Ninemile Training Camp in Missoula. The other was in the Methow Valley in Washington's North Cascades: the Winthrop base which would later be named the North Cascades Smokejumper Base (NCSB). In 1941, jumpers put out nine fires and the program seemed primed for expansion.

That December the Japanese attacked Pearl Harbor.

World War II could easily have spelled the end of smokejumping. Everything the program required, the armed forces

needed more urgently: young men, aircraft, funding, even silk
parachutes.

So many jumpers entered the military that the only way to
keep the program afloat was to train conscientious objectors,
many of them Mennonites and Quakers.

Luckily for us, the enemy turned forest fires into a matter
of national security.

Over a period of six months in 1944 and 1945, roughly
ninety-three hundred *fûsen bakudan*, or "balloon bombs," lifted
off from a beach on Honshu, Japan. Each balloon was thirty-
three feet in diameter, made of laminated mulberry paper filled
with hydrogen, and carried up to a thousand pounds of incendi-
ary devices or explosives suspended underneath.

They were designed to ride the high-altitude jet stream
across the Pacific, with automatic altitude controls. After three
days, when they would likely be over the United States, a timer
dropped the bomb to spread fear and fire. In the war effort,
wood went to everything from packing crates to gunstocks,
making our forests huge strategic natural reserves.

The balloons may have been the first intercontinental
weapons ever used, the warfare equivalent of a Hail Mary pass.
About three hundred of them turned up from Alaska to Mexico
and as far east as Michigan. The government tried to keep them
out of the news, to avoid panic and to keep the Japanese from
knowing whether they were effective or not.

Only one actually started a fire. Another got tangled in the
power lines of the Hanford Engineer Works in Washington,
which produced the plutonium for the atomic bomb used at
Nagasaki. It caused a power outage but didn't explode.

To counter the threat, the army turned to the all-black 555th Parachute Infantry Battalion, otherwise known as the Triple Nickles. These three hundred brave African American men went through parajumper training and were sent all the way to Europe—where they weren't allowed to fight because of their race.

Instead, the Triple Nickles were sent back home and retrained as smokejumpers, with a focus on finding and disposing of the balloon bombs. The same day they boarded the train to Oregon for training, a third balloon bomb exploded in southern Oregon, killing a pregnant woman and five children on a Sunday school outing. They were the only fatalities caused by the enemy in the continental United States during the entire war.

As part of the Firefly Project, the Triple Nickles made more than twelve hundred fire jumps and worked on thirty-six forest fires in the Pacific Northwest. They found a few bombs, too. Private First Class Malvin L. Brown, who died after a fall during a tree letdown, was the first smokejumper fatality.

Their efforts made smokejumping one of the first racially integrated jobs in America. Still, the men of the 555th weren't allowed in many bars, hotels, or restaurants. They were denied live ammo for rifle training and forbidden from mingling with white soldiers, which even enemy POWs could do.

The battalion was eventually absorbed into the 82nd Airborne shortly before President Harry Truman ordered the U.S. military desegregated in 1948. The Triple Nickles served in more airborne units, in peace and war, than any other parachute group in history.

THE WAR YEARS SPURRED improvements in jump gear. Chet Derry, one of the first jumpers, worked with his brother Frank to invent a better chute. In 1941, with the increasing shortage of Asian silk due to the Japanese invasion of Asia, the Forest Service turned to procuring nylon parachutes from the military—rejects that did not meet military contract specs. Chet and Frank modified the flat circular parachute by creating two slots (openings) which provided improved performance and steerability. The Derry slotted chute was easier to control and opened more gently, better for both canopy and jumper.

A static line system, where parachutes are deployed automatically by a line attached inside the plane, was developed so jumpers wouldn't have to worry about rip cords. (The first smokejumper static line was a fifteen-foot mule halter rope Earl Cooley found in a corral.)

A somewhat more refined version was in heavy use on the night of June 5, 1944, over northern France. The first part of the Normandy invasion consisted of a wave of paratroopers from the U.S. 82nd and 101st Airborne Divisions, over thirteen thousand men, who parachuted behind German lines the night before the beach landings.

Four years earlier, Major William C. Lee had visited the jumper training camp at Seeley Lake, Montana. He was impressed and used much of what he saw when he created the 101st Airborne Division in 1942 and commanded it as a major general.

Together with the 82nd Airborne, the 101st played a critical role in the success of D-day. Medical issues kept Lee from making the jump over Normandy himself, but some of his troops yelled his name when they jumped: "Bill Lee!"

Jumpers still do occasionally, out of respect.

By the end of the war, 220 trained jumpers were stationed in Oregon, Idaho, and Montana. The age range was expanded to be eighteen to thirty-five and included many former World War II paratroopers.

The jump program had survived the war and was starting to gain national attention. Four Missoula jumpers flew to Washington, D.C., to make a demonstration jump on the White House lawn, a stunt to signal the launch of a new forest fire prevention campaign. Things were looking up.

Then on August 5, 1949, disaster struck in a remote Montana canyon whose name would become part of firefighting history: Mann Gulch.

CHAPTER 5

THE MANN GULCH FIRE started on August 5, 1949, when
lightning sparked a wildfire along the Missouri River near
Helena, Montana. A planeload of fifteen smokejumpers led by
foreman Wagner Dodge was dispatched from Missoula. Thirteen of the jumpers were between seventeen and twenty-three
years old.

They found a relatively small blaze burning on the south
side of the canyon mouth. At 3:10 P.M. the crew landed about
half a mile up canyon from the fire. (First-generation jumper
Earl Cooley was the spotter.) They were joined by James Harrison, a fire guard from a nearby campground.

Dodge didn't like the look of the fire and directed the crew
down the canyon toward the river, away from the visible flames.

They thought the route would put them in a position to
attack the fire with the river at their backs. But as they hiked,
their view below was obscured by ridges. When they got about
halfway down they were shocked to suddenly discover the fire
burning below them on both sides of the canyon. Somehow—

and it is still debated today how the fire got there—a combination of high winds and embers had spread flames across the canyon's mouth, cutting off the route to the river.

Dodge knew instantly what to do: he ordered the men to turn around and hike back up the gulch as fast as possible. They stumbled up the rocky hillside to what they hoped was safety on the bare rocks on the ridge top. The slope grew steeper, slowing their progress but speeding up the fire. Twenty-foot flames tore up the hillside at almost eight miles an hour behind them.

The crew dropped their tools when the fire was about a hundred yards back. In desperation, Dodge stopped and pulled a pack of matches from his pocket. The men thought the boss had gone crazy as he knelt and lit the grass at his feet on fire.

The flames were now fifty yards behind them, less than a minute away.

Dodge's fire swept ahead through the dry grass, clearing a patch the size of a small room. He told his men to get inside the burned area, that it was their only hope. But the roar of the fire drowned out his voice, the idea of an escape fire was counterintuitive, and they were too frightened to think straight.

"To hell with that, I'm getting out of here!" someone shouted. Dodge lay in the burned grass just as the flames arrived.

Dodge's quick thinking saved his life. The other men continued sprinting up the slope, where they met a twelve-foot-high band of rock guarding the top of the ridge.

Walter Rumsey and Robert Sallee scrambled through a crevice in the rimrock and found shelter in a rock slide on the far side. They and Dodge were the only ones out of the sixteen on-site who lived.

Two more jumpers also made it to safety, but were so badly burned they died of their wounds.

The blaze raged for another five days and took 450 men to put out. It cost thirteen lives, including James Harrison, the fire guard who had quit smokejumping the year before because it was too dangerous. One body was so badly charred that rescuers at first mistook it for a tree stump.

The story of the twelve jumpers, the first to ever die on a fire, made national news. A feature in *Life* magazine portrayed them as young, brave, and doomed, like so many men in the war that had just ended. Hollywood had *Red Skies of Montana*, still the only decent movie about smokejumpers, in theaters by 1952.

Two years later, President Eisenhower personally opened the new aerial fire depot in Missoula. Even though it took a tragedy, the government was now committed to smokejumping for the long term. The Forest Service improved jumper training in weather, safety, and communications. It also poured money into the scientific study of fire behavior, leading to the creation of the Interagency Fire Science Laboratory in Missoula.

Francis Lufkin had become base manager at NCSB, a position he held for three decades. He made fifty-seven jumps and saw two of his sons go on to become jumpers before he died in 1998. He received a Presidential Award from Lyndon B. Johnson—not for fire fighting, but for the economy. As his son tells it, he saved the United States of America something like a million dollars in firefighting costs. It's safe to say there wouldn't be an American smokejumper program without him.

The Bureau of Land Management started its own smokejumping program in Alaska in 1959. As always, the BLM had a lot of land to cover; initially seventeen jumpers were responsible for an area the size of Texas. California was the next state to get a Forest Service jump base. Today there are seven Forest Service bases in California, Idaho, Montana, Oregon, and Washington, and two BLM bases in Boise and Fairbanks.

By the 1960s, the smokejumper program counted four hundred jumpers. This was a decade of change, including in the world of fighting wildfire.

In 1963, the deployment bag ("D-bag"; and, yes, you read that right) chute system was officially adopted. Before, the sudden shock of the parachute opening could pop your helmet off or even knock you unconscious, especially if you were in the wrong position.

With the D-bag, the chute comes out of the backpack still packed inside a small bag. This leaves time for the parachute lines and risers—the nylon straps that attach the lines to the harness—to straighten out before the chute inflates. It's a much softer opening, and less prone to malfunctions.

That same year, a jumper made it to the top of the world. On May 22, Willi Unsoeld, an alumnus of the base at Cave Junction, Oregon, climbed Mount Everest's West Ridge with Tom Hornbein. They weren't the first Americans on the summit—Jim Whittaker had made it by the standard South Col route three weeks earlier—but they did pioneer a much more difficult route. By descending via the South Col, Unsoeld and Hornbein also made the first traverse of the mountain. In the process they had to spend the night at twenty-eight thousand feet without sleeping bags or tents, which cost Unsoeld nine toes.

Another Cave Junction jumper eventually upped the ante even further. In 1971, Stuart Roosa, the command module pilot for *Apollo 14*, became one of only twenty-four people ever to travel to the moon.

By now the Forest Service had been operating under a policy of total fire suppression for more than half a century. The public mostly agreed, thanks to characters like Smokey Bear and Bambi, whose nightmare-inducing forest fire scene traumatized a generation.

By the 1960s and 1970s, however, scientists and forest managers were starting to rethink the practice. Total fire suppression wasn't healthy for forest ecosystems, it turned out, and it didn't always make economic sense, either. Prescribed fires started to be used more often, and some natural fires were allowed to burn, provided lives and property weren't at risk.

The era of the career smokejumper had begun. Early jumpers were often recent vets or college students working for a summer or two. Now they were sticking around longer and moving on to permanent jobs in the Forest Service. Some eventually took on positions of authority, which was good because no one knows how to use a specialized resource like smokejumpers better than a former jumper.

The program was still small, selective, and highly effective, so maybe it was inevitable that it acquired a reputation that was part real, part folklore. At the same time, a pervasive anti-jumper attitude was hard to shake. Local forest managers didn't always appreciate how smokejumpers literally dropped in, worked circles around local crews, and then disappeared.

During the Vietnam War, there was one group who was grateful for the smokejumpers' unusual roster of talents. Vietnam was the first war that saw the widespread use of helicopters for tactical and rescue missions. Paratroopers—many of whom were former jumpers—only made one official combat jump during the entire conflict, in 1967.

But over the border in Laos, the CIA had been busily (and secretly) helping Hmong tribes fight communist forces for years. That meant dropping thousands of tons of supplies from planes flown by Air America, the agency's clandestine airline. They needed people who knew how to drop cargo from low-flying planes, accurately, in rough terrain, under urgent and less-than-ideal conditions.

Who else would you call? Jumpers were physically fit, didn't get airsick, and were trained to work without much supervision and improvise when necessary. Plus they were civilians, so nothing they did could be considered an official act of war.

More than fifty smokejumpers eventually ended up doing covert paramilitary missions for the CIA or Air America in Laos, Vietnam, Thailand, and Cambodia. The work paid well, and it wasn't exactly a secret in jumper circles. There was a lot of wink-wink-nudge-nudge in the spring, when guys would come back from a season in "Alaska" or "Maine" with sunburns and jungle rot between their toes.

The CIA work turned out to be even more dangerous than fighting wildfire: nine jumpers died on duty with the agency.

Another former NCSB jumper, George (Ken) Sisler, went to Southeast Asia as a twenty-nine-year-old lieutenant with the Studies and Observations Group (SOG), a top-secret special ops unit. (A few years earlier, Sisler had won the won the National Collegiate Skydiving Championship with one leg in a cast.)

In February 1967, Sisler was in Laos on an intelligence mission when over one hundred North Vietnamese soldiers attacked his platoon on three sides. Sisler ran through enemy fire to rescue two wounded men. In the process he shot and killed three enemy soldiers and destroyed a machine gun with a grenade.

As more of his companions fell wounded, he counterattacked alone, firing and throwing grenades, forcing the enemy back. He was directing air strikes when he was shot and killed. Sisler was awarded a posthumous Medal of Honor, the first given to a military intelligence officer. In addition, a U.S. Navy supply ship, the USNS *Sisler (T-AKR-311)*, was named after him in 1997.

Back home, a more public event drew official attention to smokejumpers, at least briefly. On Thanksgiving Eve, 1971, a man who identified himself as Dan Cooper (later misnamed "D. B. Cooper" by the press) bought a plane ticket from Portland to Seattle.

This was a time when airline security was notoriously lax. So when Cooper told a flight attendant he had a bomb in his briefcase, nobody was that surprised—this kind of thing happened surprisingly often back then.

Cooper politely demanded $200,000 cash and four parachutes. He paid for two bourbons and insisted the stewardess keep the change. He let most of the crew disembark in Seattle and had the Boeing 727 take off again heading south. Somewhere over southwest Washington, Cooper cranked down the rear stairs and leaped into the stormy darkness carrying twenty-one pounds of cash.

One of the biggest manhunts in Northwest history followed. FBI agents visited the North Cascades base twice, looking for anyone who had the nerve and know-how to pull off a stunt like Cooper's. Base manager Francis Lufkin didn't think the guy was a jumper. Cooper had chosen an older parachute over a professional sport chute and had picked a reserve chute that was clearly marked as nonfunctional, for demonstrations only.

And not even a smokejumper was crazy enough to jump at night, in the rain, into rugged timber country, wearing loafers and a trench coat. The general consensus was, whoever Cooper was, he probably killed himself jumping out of that plane.

The only clue anyone ever found was a $5,800 bundle of the ransom money that washed out of a sandbar in the Columbia River in 1980. Despite numerous alleged sightings, Cooper's true fate remained a mystery. His crime is still the only unsolved skyjacking in U.S. history.

At the height of the Cold War, smokejumping briefly opened a door between the United States and the Soviet Union. Russia has more forests than any other country, a fifth of the world's total, and the Soviets had started their own jump program back in 1936.

In 1976, jumpers Bill Moody and Doug Bird traveled to the USSR for a month on a technical exchange program to test the Soviet parachute system. The Forest Service's FS-10 canopy was due for an upgrade. The Russian system used a small drogue chute to deploy the canopy instead of a static line, and it was more maneuverable and descended more slowly.

Moody had become the base manager of NCSB four years earlier, fifteen years into his thirty-three year jump career. The Russians were very friendly, he told me, genuinely interested in the Americans and their training and equipment. Nightly vodka toasts helped break down the cultural barriers.

During their monthlong visit, Moody made two jumps over eastern Siberia, both with a Russian jump partner. The first was with all American gear and the second was with the Russian system. Doug Bird watched from the plane, a historic (by our standards) Antonov An-2 biplane.

The jumps went well, and the next year Nikolai Andreev, chief of aerial fire operations for the USSR, visited NCSB to make a formal presentation of a Soviet chute system and jump-suit and to make a jump of his own. After the visit they gave us their parachute system. The main round parachute, the "Lesnik" Forester, was adapted by the MTDC (at that time called MEDC) into the FS-12 chute that the Forest Service used through the 1990s. Bill Moody sent the drogue portion of their system up to Alaska, where the BLM adopted the Forester drogue for their ram-air systems.

Budget cuts and an objective of centralization in the late 1970s and early 1980s led the Forest Service to close the jump base in Cave Junction, Oregon, one of the four original jump bases. The bases in Boise, Idaho, and LaGrande, Oregon, were also shuttered. Boise was later reopened as a BLM base. The Forest Service came near to closing the NCSB, even to the point of carting away the sewing machines used to make har-nesses and other gear. Nevertheless, the birthplace of American smokejumping stayed open. In the end, jumper numbers were reduced by close to one hundred.

Other changes were happening too. In 1981, Deanne Shul-man, a former hotshot, finished rookie training at McCall and became the country's first female smokejumper.

Like any major change, opening the ranks to women caused some debate. Some people felt some bases compromised their standards to get women through training—things like relaxing the minimum height requirement and, eventually by the early 90s, adding two more sizes of canopies and changing how the PT test was administered.

If you're a jumper, it doesn't matter to me who you are, what your gender is, what race you are, what you look like. If you can pass the rookie training, get your shit on and let's go.

The same year Shulman made her first fire jump, Charlotte Larson became the first female smokejumper pilot.

SINCE MANN GULCH, SMOKEJUMPING had changed. In the early days, each base was fairly independent, free to test different strategies and develop their own gear. But in the 1960s, base managers and the Missoula Equipment Development Center (now known as the Missoula Technology Development Center, or MTDC) began having annual workshops which resulted in a more national approach to equipment development, smoke-jumper-related policy and standardization of training and jump procedures. Some bases continued to operate "independently" when they were not satisfied with the slow pace or course that MEDC and the national office were taking—especially true in regards to main parachute development.

Jumpers had proved they could do things no one else could, and fire managers had learned how to use their unique skills to the best advantage. Jumper training was standardized, safety systems were refined, and for half a century there were no burnover fatalities.

That changed in 1994 when the Storm King fire killed four-teen firefighters, including three smokejumpers.

Everyone in the wildland firefighting world remembers where they were when they heard the news. At the time I was with the Kernville crew and didn't know any jumpers person-ally, but I would in the years to come. Five years after Storm King, I was more determined than ever to become a smoke-jumper—cracked leg or not.

CHAPTER 6

AFTER THE DOCTOR SHOWED me the x-ray, my next medical appointment was with a specialist in the same building.

I cursed myself the whole way over. How could I get this close and screw it up?

In the specialist's office I told him I was about to start training to be a smokejumper. He gave my leg a quick exam and shook his head.

"You cannot go," he said in a heavy Asian accent. He explained that if I landed on the leg wrong, the bone could snap completely.

"I have to do this," I said, almost pleading.

He thought for a moment, then told me to roll up my pant leg. He started to probe around the injury with his fingers. Before I could react, he dug a thumb right into the most tender spot.

I clutched my fists and gritted my teeth and fought the crazy urge to rabbit-punch him right on the top of his head. My eyes watered like I had just gotten punched in the nose.

He looked up at me and nodded like I had passed some kind of test.

"Okay," he said. "You go, but it will hurt."

I left the office with a slight limp, a customized training plan, instructions to take strong anti-inflammatories, and a soft cast to keep my leg from getting worse.

The next hurdle was the mandatory government physical. My leg would have gotten me instantly disqualified, so I kept my mouth shut.

In the months before training started, I tried to learn as much about smokejumping as I could. I found a few writeups here and there in books at the fire station, and there was one documentary I found and watched, over and over. (This was back before everything was on Google or YouTube.)

Anything to give me a leg up, so to speak. There wasn't much.

Every day I had to face down a little voice of self-doubt in the back of my head, the one that wouldn't stop asking: *Are you good enough? Strong enough? Brave enough? Smart enough?*

I'd heard stories about firefighters I knew, guys who were tough as hell, washing out of jumper training in the first week. Even on their first day.

It dawned on me that making the cut wasn't just about being in top physical shape. The mental component was just as important, if not more. Having some common sense and luck didn't hurt. But you had to be tough *and* sharp enough to pass.

Was I? I asked myself this question a lot in the run-up to rookie training.

Finally I reached what you might call a mental point of no

return. *I will pass this program,* I promised myself, *because the only way I'm leaving is in the back of an ambulance.*

Two more calls came in with offers to join rookie classes at other bases. One was from Redding, in Northern California, which I politely turned down since I had already committed to NCSB.

The other offer really pissed me off. After the usual chit-chat, the base manager asked something that caught me by surprise. "Where does your last name come from?" he said.

Having worked for the government for over ten years, I knew about affirmative action. I understood the thinking behind it, but in practice I thought it was bullshit.

I had seen too many people given jobs they weren't qualified for. Sometimes this led to situations that put people's lives at risk.

The only thing that should matter is having the skills and experience to be a good firefighter—period.

"I'm Puerto Rican," I said mildly.

"I'd like to offer you a job," he said. Nothing about my training, or if I was in good shape, any of the normal smokejumper questions. Not even whether I could cook a decent plate of black beans and rice.

I didn't have to think twice.

"No thank you, sir." There was a moment of silence.

I explained I had already committed to NCSB. But I think he got the message that I wasn't going to take a job just because of my nationality or the color of my skin.

The call ended with a simple, "Thank you."

IT WAS A LONG, slow drive to Redmond, Oregon, in my 1974 Econoline van, with its top speed of sixty miles per hour (downhill, when aided by a tailwind).

Jumper training can last for five or six weeks, and this year—1999—the rookie classes from NCSB and Redmond were training together. Part of the instruction would be held at each base. Redmond was first.

I got there on a Saturday, a day early. The first jumper I met as I stepped out of my van was a big, serious-looking Native American guy with a chest that looked as wide as my one-ton camper van. He showed me the barracks and told me where to go for the first meeting the following afternoon.

Other candidates drifted in throughout the day, close to two dozen men and women in all. We made small talk and sized each other up. Everyone was between their midtwenties and early thirties. Each had at least two seasons of wildland firefighting experience, just to be here. Most had five to ten. There were more hotshots than anything else.

All clearly badasses, just to make it this far. Beyond that, my fellow trainees were a mystery.

None of us had any idea what we were in for.

AT A QUICK BRIEFING on Sunday afternoon, the lead instructor took roll call. There were six candidates from NCSB and another half dozen or more from Redmond. When he got to my name, he looked up. "I heard about you," he said.

Great, I thought. *We haven't even started yet, and I'm already on the head trainer's Christmas list.*

This was going to be an interesting month.

After going over the basic rules for training—when and where to show up, what to wear—he told us to go get a good night's sleep. We'd need it.

The next morning was the minimum physical standards test, the one I'd been preparing myself for for so long I'd almost forgotten what life was like before. If you don't pass, you can't even start training.

First came the calisthenics: at least seven chin-ups, twenty-five push-ups and forty-five sit-ups in a row. The trainers watched us like hawks to make sure there was no cheating: pull-ups with palms forward, no kipping, push-ups all the way down to the ground.

That was the easy part.

Next we had to run a mile and a half in eleven minutes or less. My leg throbbed as we jogged over the flat course. Even so I made the cutoff with time to spare. Remember, these are the bare minimums. Some guys are known to have run a mile and a half in 7:25.

Last was the infamous pack-out test: a three-mile hike, carrying 110 pounds, in under ninety minutes. They called it an "easy" pack test, since it was on level ground. Like the rest, it was pass or fail. No second chance.

I crammed my pack full to bursting with random gear until it weighed enough. I tried not to think about what happened back in my parents' workout room the first time I had tried to pick up a pack that big.

All those years of effort came down to the next hour and a half. The timer started and we took off. The straps dug into my shoulders as I tried to hit the perfect pace: fast enough to finish in time, slow enough not to flame out too soon.

Aside from some aches in my leg, I actually felt pretty good as we plodded along. I crossed the finish line in a little over an hour. Not the fastest in the group, but not the slowest, either.

One guy didn't make the ninety-minute cutoff. Just like that, he was gone.

A little over a month isn't very long to absorb even the basics of something as complex as smokejumping. In a way that was the point. The brief intensity of the training reflected the job itself.

On a fire, there's no time to putz around. Since 1939 jumper training has been designed to show who can think on their feet, act quickly and decisively, without having every little thing explained to death.

Our instructors were all experienced jumpers in senior positions that are collectively known as "overhead" at jump bases. Five or six of them shepherded us through the whole program, with other trainers coming and going as the weeks went by.

That first day, after the minimum standards test, each trainer gave a short briefing that was part introduction, part pep talk. Most of it boiled down to three simple things: listen to what your trainers say, do what you're told, and give one hundred and ten percent.

As one trainer told us, "You need to be heads-up from the minute you pour milk on your cereal every morning. Smell your milk, guys!"

When they were done, the air felt charged, like before a storm.

"Training has now started!" one trainer shouted. "You have two minutes to get your PT clothes on. Move it, rooks!"

We scrambled for the door, pushing and shoving, as the instructors shouted, "Go, go, go!"

The first week consisted mostly of fitness tests designed to push us to our limits. Every day included at least two PT sessions. There were endless calisthenics and runs.

We did another pack-out test, this one with a four-hour time limit, over terrain that got steeper and rougher as the course went on. Luckily our packs were lighter: only ninety-five pounds.

Trainers stood along the course to track our progress and offer commentary. "You can give up any time," one said. "We'll carry your pack for you. We'll even help you pack and find you another job."

"Just take a break," said another, waving a psychedelic-looking drink. "Who wants a milkshake?" The word made my mouth water. I couldn't stop thinking about the malted shakes my dad used to make.

Then I passed another trainee writhing in the dirt with the worst leg cramps I had ever seen. That got milkshakes off my mind for a little while. He ended up washing out that week.

The instructors were expert at finding that fine line between maximum effort and putting someone in the hospital. But it wasn't just suffering for its own sake. The physical side of jumper training shows who can keep going and going and going, long past the point you thought was your limit back in the normal world.

Can you keep pushing through even though you're hurt, sleep deprived, hungry, dehydrated, in the middle of nowhere, with a wall of flames or a Sasquatch on your ass? Those who can't—often up to half of each class—wash out. Sometimes they give up and quit the program, wash out due to medical or physical issues, or they're thanked for their efforts and advised to try out another year.

Nearly half the group was gone by the first Thursday. It happened quickly. There wasn't any ritual, like in fire academies or the military. The person just disappeared. You'd just notice someone's gear piled in a corner, or an empty seat, or someone's name missing on the list at roll call one morning.

Sometimes you saw it coming, if someone was lagging behind the pack on runs or just doing stupid shit. Those were the ones the trainers focused their attention on, and they usually didn't last long.

I learned never to categorize or underestimate someone. Some of the biggest, fittest athletes alive have keeled over on the first day or week of training. Others who just squeak in at either end of the size limits—five feet to six feet five inches tall, 120 to 200 pounds—end up jumping successfully for years.

Dropping out of something you put so much effort into can be mentally crushing. Many candidates who wash out end up pulling out of the fire service completely.

One afternoon near the end of the first week, I entered the bunkhouse to find one of my classmates, a stocky guy, sitting on the floor in the hall with his back against the wall. His head was down and he was clearly upset. He had just failed one of the PT tests.

All of us were at our limits. No one had time or energy left over for sympathy, no late-night bonding sessions or hand-holding. At that point it was still every person for him- or herself.

I just walked past him to my room and closed the door.

As they put us through the paces, our trainers would offer occasional reminders to keep things in perspective. "Give yourself a round of applause at the end of the day," they said. "You finished today, but you might be gone tomorrow. Have a good night, ladies and gentlemen."

Not exactly encouraging. But it was the truth.

To keep the pain and swelling down in my leg I was popping Advil and Relafen, a prescription anti-inflammatory, like they were candy.

To make things worse, the entire arch on my right foot turned into one big blister by the first weekend, the result of a poor choice of socks on one of the pack tests. One morning before a PT run, a trainer pointed at my shoe.

"Ramos!" he barked. "What's up with your foot?"

A faint red stain was seeping through the white material. I wished I'd had the foresight to buy some damned red shoes.

A few days later my foot started sprouting white lumps like alien pods. The blister had become infected. I called my pops for advice, and I could hear the concern in his voice.

"Son, if that gets any worse, you're going to have to get some assistance right away," he said. Meaning see a doctor.

"No way," I said. "If I do that, I'm out."

"Well, then you're going to have to clean it out yourself," he said.

I knew he was right. After I hung up, I closed my door and sat on the edge of my bed with a bottle of hydrogen peroxide.

I stuck a toothbrush between my teeth, silently cursing those shitty socks. I was so mad I wanted to howl, but I didn't want anyone to hear me. I held my breath and dumped the peroxide under the infected flap of skin.

Leaning back on the bed, I wished I could punch something nice and satisfying but all I could do was bite on my toothbrush. Holy shit, that stung. After a few more pours, the pain ebbed and I scrubbed the blisters out as best I could.

I wished I had a few bottles of saline to wash the wound out. But if I had asked for any, or gotten caught trying to sneak some out, it would have meant a first-class ride to the doctor—and a ticket home.

Irrigation was the key. It took a few more days, but the alien pod infestation finally cleared up.

BY THE SECOND WEEK of training the days settled into a carefully structured pattern. After roll call and morning PT, the rest of the time was divided between classroom instruction and field exercises where we put our new knowledge to the test.

You learned damn quick to stay awake in class, which was especially hard right after lunch. If the instructors caught you dozing off, they'd reward you with long wall sits or some other punishing exercise.

The day typically ended with still more PT, anything from trail running to tree climbing, maybe with a few dozen push-ups and lunges thrown in for good measure. We always brought our running clothes on field exercises, since the trainers could always decide to drop us off in the middle of the woods with nothing more than a direction to go and a loose promise to pick us up again in the vehicle. Eventually.

We learned about the standard Forest Service smokejumper parachute, the FS-14. The simple, round design goes back to before World War II and has been perfected over decades of use. It does exactly what it is meant to: get a jumper safely to the ground in some of the roughest terrain anywhere.

Imagine a huge radio tower chopped off about forty feet from the ground. That's what the exit tower looked like, and we spent most of the second week of training either climbing it or jumping off it.

The top level had a mock-up of an airplane door for practicing our exits. A good exit is critical. If you don't leave the plane correctly, it can cause a chute malfunction, make you miss your jump spot, or worse.

The trainers watched as we double-timed it up the stairs in full jump gear, clipped in our static lines, and assumed the correct prejump position. When you jumped through the fake door, everything else was as close to real as possible, from the few brief seconds of free fall to the shock that followed, hard enough to make my neck and jaw hurt for days.

Instead of a parachute, you ended up dangling from a long cable that slid you down to the ground like a zipline. After landing and unclipping, you hoofed it back to the tower, trotted up two flights of stairs, and did it again, over and over, dozens of times a day.

The middle tower level was for practicing tree letdowns. Smokejumpers often don't have the luxury of nice, open landing zones—especially in the Pacific Northwest, where steep mountainsides and old-growth forests are the norm.

If you end up landing in a tree, your next job is get to the ground safely. I already knew how to rappel, but doing it from a parachute stuck in the top of a hundred-foot Douglas fir was another story.

Every jumper carries a 150-foot letdown rope coiled in a leg pocket. On the tower we learned how to anchor the rope to the tightest side of our parachute riser, the webbing that connects the harness to the parachute.

The next step is to detach from the canopy by pulling on two metal releases called Capewells, one on each side. Then all you have to do is rappel down. In a tree that means navigating branches and foliage.

Everything has to be smooth and easy. If your canopy isn't hung up securely—ideally over the very top of the tree like a pillowcase on a pole—you have to anchor the letdown rope to the tree itself. The last thing you want is to Capewell too early and end up with a parachute shroud wrapped around your neck, which resulted in a fatality in 1966.

Sometimes you can do everything right and still find yourself dangling. In 1970, an NCSB rookie ended his third jump in the crown of an old-growth monster in the Olympic National Park. When he rappelled, he found the end of his 240-foot letdown rope was still 30 feet off the ground. A buddy had to help him swing over to a nearby tree.

We also practiced climbing trees to retrieve parachutes and cargo. Our instructors showed us how to strap on metal heel spurs and wrap a steel-cored flipline around the trunk. By flipping it upward, you climb the trunk like a telephone lineman.

As with everything, the instructors gave us a quick explanation and demonstration, then stepped back to watch us work it out for ourselves. They critiqued our technique and timed us up and down.

Tick tock, tick tock.

Of all the tower exercises, the one that almost did me in was at the very bottom.

Most jumper injuries come from bad landings. Even if you hit your landing spot, with an FS-14 on a normal day, you are still moving up to eight to ten miles an hour forward with a descent rate of approximately ten feet per second. To absorb the shock with your whole body, you do a controlled tumble called a parachute landing fall, or PLF.

The lowest level of the tower had a pair of platforms, five and seven feet off the ground. We used them to practice PLFs by jumping off and rolling in the dirt.

It's hard enough remembering everything you're supposed to do as the ground rushes up: first and foremost, face into the wind. Don't forget to keep your legs together, bend your knees, tuck your elbows in, and rotate your body to spread the impact across your thigh, your butt, and the side of your back.

It's even harder when you know one wrong move could break your tibia. I couldn't help favoring my left leg when I hit the ground. It got so bad an instructor pulled me aside for some one-on-one training.

"Like this, Ramos!" he said, demonstrating how to do it correctly.

Up to this point I had somehow kept my condition a secret. But now I was clearly falling behind. Next week we would start jumping for real, and doing a good PLF was one of the mandatory requirements for moving on.

One day after yet another shit show, one of the instructors from NCSB came to my van and asked what was up. I came clean about my injury. "I'm pushing as hard as I can," I said.

His answer was brutal in its honesty. "I don't care," he said. "You better pick it up. On a fire it doesn't matter if you're hurt. You need to perform. I want all NCSB up front on every PT!"

A few days later, the NCSB base manager asked me what was going on. I told him the truth and held my breath.

"Well, Ramos, maybe you should try next year," he said. My heart lurched.

"No sir," I muttered. "I'm not leaving."

He didn't waste words. "Then get your ass out there and fix it."

I didn't know if I left that talk with extra brownie points for hanging in there, or one step closer to going home. They could easily have chosen to wash me out, if only for the liability. All it would have taken was one order to get an x-ray and it would be *adiós* Ramos.

I just knew the only way I was leaving was on a backboard. I wanted to provide extraordinary service to my country, and this was the path I had chosen to do my part.

When I get stressed, it's hard for me to eat or sleep. The night before the practical tests we had to pass to move on to jump operations, I managed to cram down some Gardenburgers. I still can't stand veggie burgers to this day.

We all passed our practicals on the second Friday. "If you have questions, ask them now," the instructors said by way of congratulations. "Because come Monday morning, you will be on your own, folks."

CHAPTER 7

THE MORNING OF OUR first fire jump, one of the trainers rolled a TV and a VCR into the training room and hit play. Up popped a scene of a scruffy guy scribbling on a blackboard, babbling nonsense about planes and parachutes.

Wait—was that Kevin Costner? I knew this movie: *Fandango.* This was where the dude pulls his rip cord in midair and finds his pack is full of dirty laundry.

We trainees glanced at one another. It was funny and a little crazy. *This couldn't be the whole briefing,* I thought. But when the movie clip was over, the order came to suit up—for real this time.

Ten minutes later we were taxiing down the runway. The plane's cabin filled with the fumes of jet-A and the earsplitting *waa-waa-waa* of the Sherpa's engine.

Originally designed as a small military transport, the twin-engined Shorts C-23 Sherpa has flown with the U.S. Army and Air Force in places like Iraq and Afghanistan. It isn't a pretty plane, and it's not especially powerful or maneuverable. But its boxy body is roomy inside. Some people call it a "Flying Winnebago."

As the wheels left the ground, it hit me that this was a one-way trip. For the first time in my life, I was taking off in a plane that I wouldn't land in.

I looked around the cabin at the other trainees. On every face, half hidden behind a metal mesh face mask, was a look of solemn concentration.

After the first wave of washouts, we had slowly started to bond as a group. Two weeks of eating, sleeping, showering, and suffering side by side will do that. We were learning how we each responded to stress, who was good in the classroom or the tower, who was willing to circle back around after a run to make sure everyone else was in. People could still wash out—and they would—but we had done well to have made it this far together.

I looked at Hillbilly, another NCSB trainee whose absurd sense of humor was a lot like mine. He had experience as a hotshot and helitack. Usually he was a regular Mel Blanc, cracking us up with his many impressions. Right now he was quiet, though. His eyes were wide with anticipation.

It only took a few minutes to reach the jump spot, a large open meadow in south-central Oregon. The pilot started circling at twenty-five hundred feet, a thousand feet higher than the standard fire jump altitude.

Wind howled through the open door as the spotter threw out a set of streamers. The twenty-foot strips of colored crepe paper are weighted with sand at one end to fall at the same speed as a jumper under a parachute. They mark the landing zone and show the descent rate, critical info for a safe landing. Most important, they indicate which way the wind is blowing, both up high and near the ground.

From the back of the lineup I watched my classmates leave the plane one by one in a whoosh and a cloud of dust. We were doing our first jumps alone for safety.

Everyone's exit seemed to go smoothly. Even if you made it out safely, though, there were still plenty of ways a parachute could malfunction. In class we had gone over every one in detail.

Your main canopy could not deploy at all—say, if you forgot to clip your static line, which has happened. Or it could deploy but not inflate, leaving you plummeting under a "full streamer." In both cases your best option was to pull the handle that deployed your reserve chute, a smaller canopy packed in a case on your chest.

A main chute that only partly inflated gave you more options and a little more time. A line wrapped over the top of the canopy—called a "Mae West" for the twin-peaked shape it made—might come free with a good yank. An inside-out canopy, an inversion, was rare, but sometimes you could still steer one to a safe landing. A broken steering line meant you'd have to do riser turns, pulling on your riser instead of the line itself, which works but much more slowly.

For other problems, like a torn canopy, it was your call, depending on your rate of descent, whether to ride it out or deploy your reserve.

The spotter's voice yanked my mind back to the present. I was next in line.

The jump door checklist passed in a blur, so familiar from all the endless training, and before I knew it I was airborne.

THE NEXT FOUR SECONDS were pure controlled excitement. Back in 1999 we still jumped in the pike position with our bodies straight and at a slight angle, like paratroopers still are trained to do to this day.

I watched my feet rise toward the horizon as I counted out loud: "Jump thousand, two thousand, three thousand, four thousand, check my canopy, check my jump partner, check my jump spot."

The parachute deployed with a snap, right on time. I'll never forget the sudden, total silence and clarity, seeing the canopy against the blue sky overhead.

My canopy looked in good shape. I looked down for the streamers that marked the jump spot. The voice of an instructor crackled over my radio. "Left toggle. Ok, now right toggle. Half brakes." I worked the high-tech wooden handles that steered the parachute and controlled my speed.

Before I knew it I was coming in face into the wind and my feet touched the grass. I had made my first jump.

My classmates were waiting. We traded hoots and a few high fives—I stuck with my old-school low fives—but not for long. We gathered up our gear and hustled over to where the instructors were waiting to evaluate our first qualifying jumps in excruciating detail.

Fourteen more to go.

The jumps gradually increased in difficulty. We started

jumping in pairs, in the standard two-person stick. (Smoke-jumpers leave the plane in "sticks," usually two people [a double stick] who jump one after the other, occasionally three [triple stick] or one [single stick].)

We also started jumping from only fifteen hundred feet AGL (above ground level) and into steeper and rougher terrain, aiming at landing spots that grew progressively smaller.

Every jump was analyzed from exit to descent to landing, as strictly as if we were pilots learning to land on an aircraft carrier. First you gave your account of what you thought happened, and then the trainers would say what they saw. When the accounts didn't match up, there were cameras on the ground recording everything.

It's surprising how often you'd swear you did one thing but found you did the exact opposite, like turning right in midair instead of left. It forced us to improve our situational awareness and technique. It also taught us to slow down and think through what we were doing.

As one of the smaller people in the class, I struggled with my exits. In the pike position, the rush of air kept wanting to flip me upside down. An inversion can tangle your lines or your chute.

I did invert on one jump and ended up tangled for a few seconds. Happily I was able to fix the problem before I landed.

In the late 2000s, the program switched to a cannonball-style exit position that cut down on bad exits.

SOME DAYS OF JUMP training were a blur, and others I just wanted to be over.

Eventually we all moved up to the North Cascades Smoke-jumper Base in Winthrop, Washington.

The small town sat in the long, narrow valley carved by the Methow River as it runs east and south out of the Cascades.

An old forestry, mining, and ranching center, Winthrop now draws tourists with its mountain scenery and old-timey western downtown, complete with raised wooden sidewalks and false-front buildings. One of these is the oldest legal saloon in the state: Three-Finger Jacks was named after its original owner, who lost two fingers in a marksmanship bet (which he still won, by the way).

We didn't have much time for that kind of stuff, even on our days off. By this point we were jumping every day, weather permitting. We started pairing up with the older guys, the experienced jumpers. It was a confidence booster, though they never let us forget we still had a long way to go if we wanted to stick around. There's nothing like getting ready to jump and having the other half of your stick say, "Stay the fuck away from me, rook!"

Everyone had his or her own way to deal with the stress of an upcoming jump. Some people stretched beforehand, while others preferred to hit the head or put in a dip of chewing tobacco. I usually hummed a tune to help me chill out, usually something out of the punk canon: Agent Orange, Rancid, Social Distortion.

Training was a constant mind-screw. It wouldn't be fair to call it *Full Metal Jacket*–style hazing, designed to break you down and build you back up as an unquestioning member of a cohesive unit.

It's more subtle than that, a raised eyebrow after a botched practical test, or the stone-cold look on an instructor's face followed by him scribbling who knows what in his notebook.

The lead trainer who had recognized my name the first day of training ended up riding my ass the whole time. Maybe it was because I was a heli-rappeler, or because I was a California boy from Region 5, either of which was enough to earn a spot on some jumpers' shit list. Maybe he just didn't like the way I looked, or my makeshift house on wheels. (I was living out of my van.)

In any case, it meant I had to be that much more on top of things. During our last qualifying jump, we were all understandably nervous. My exit went fine, but on the way down I heard the lead trainer's voice growling on the radio. "Who in the hell is that way out there?"

Someone was far downwind of the jump spot. I knew it wasn't me, because I could see only two other jumpers were closer.

Another trainer chimed in: "That's not Ramos, that's your guy." The wandering jumper was from Redmond, the lead trainer's home base.

Ha, I thought. *Nice try, dickhead.*

WHEN OUR QUALIFYING JUMPS were finished, the Redmond trainees went home. We knew the ordeal had to be almost over. What else could they throw at us—another run, a hike, or some other exercise in pain management we hadn't yet experienced?

People were still washing out as late as the fourth week, but the rest of us knew we had passed the big hurdle. We knew we could get bloody or sick and survive.

One morning after roll call, the assistant base manager stood up and said without preamble, "I want to congratulate you all for completing your training as the NCSB rookie class of 1999."

We looked at each other, dazed. Holy shit—we made it.

The base manager gave a quick speech. "You are rookie smokejumpers now, and you know what is expected of you," he said. "If not, we will remind you."

One by one, he gave us each a small metal pin. Our rookie jump wings. Now our names would go on the jump board for active duty.

Every fifty jumps earns you another pair of wings. My rookie pin is the most special by far.

I was awash with relief, elation, and most of all pride. To be part of the last smokejumper class of the twentieth century was an honor I couldn't put into words.

The ceremony, such as it was, was over in a few minutes. Afterward we gathered outside for PT. As always, we started jogging in a line.

"You're done, rookies," yelled a senior jumper from the parachute loft. "Stop running together!"

Everyone laughed and took off in different directions, some tripping in haste, ready to be alone for the first time in weeks, with only ourselves to answer to.

CHAPTER 8

THE CRASH COURSE OF rookie training is just the beginning of a jumper's education. Even after sixteen years I'm still learning new things all the time.

Of the many skills you pick up in your first few years, there's one that tends to surprise people: smokejumpers, as a rule, are great at sewing.

Think about it: Who's going to make and sell highly specialized equipment for a customer base of a few hundred people? No one. So we have to make all our jumpsuits, harnesses, and gear bags ourselves, from scratch. That way everything is exactly what we need—customized, tailored, and quality controlled. The designs have been handed down through generations of jumpers, yet you can still tweak them to your heart's content.

In my first few seasons, I learned that inspecting, repairing, and making your own gear is a big part of daily life between fire jumps. So is bull cooking (an old term borrowed from logging and mining camps for cleaning, maintenance, and chores), PT and ongoing training. But your life can depend on your gear, so you'd better make damn sure every piece is in good working order.

An experienced jumper can sew better than most clothing manufacturers, even with burly textiles like Kevlar and Nomex.

"Lofties" at NCSB spend their spare time in the Lufkin Parachute Loft, where industrial sewing machines clatter away and parachute canopies hang from the high ceiling like strange silky trees.

Everyone has his or her forte. Some people are good with machines, like chain saws, while others like giving tours of the base. Some, like me, are gearheads, always trying to figure out how to modify and improve every piece of clothing and equipment.

Some folks you don't want anywhere near a sewing machine, especially with materials in the $70-per-square-yard territory.

The biggest project is the jumpsuit, a totally unique garment designed for one purpose: to get you to the ground in one piece. The Kevlar outer material is so resistant to abrasion and punctures you have to cut it with a rotary textile saw. Even though you take the suit off once you're on the ground, it's still highly fire-resistant just in case. The fabric is also used in structural firefighting and can withstand 2000°F for four seconds.

For extra protection there are closed-cell foam pads for the knees, elbows, butt, and spine. Some jumpers like to wear motorcycle or hockey pads. The suit has an integrated rappel system and a high, padded protective collar. The overall effect is a combination of a knight's armor and a superhero suit.

There are tons of pockets inside and out for things like cold-weather gear, tents, extra food, whatever you want to bring. One of the extralarge pockets on each lower leg holds your letdown rope. Your pack-out bag usually goes in the other leg pocket, but some guys wear it under their jump suit or wherever else they prefer to stash it. The pack-out bag is a frameless pack that's also custom-made at the base. (The weights we deal with would blow out the seams of most commercial packs.)

If you ask me, our jumpsuits are cool as hell.

Underneath, we wear government-issue fire pants and a fire shirt made of a flame-resistant para-aramid textile blend that won't burn (like cotton does) or melt into your skin (like other synthetic fabrics) under normal conditions on the line.

More firefighters are starting to pay out of their own pockets for garments manufactured by top companies in the U.S. that use newer, high-performance, fire-resistant textiles designed to breathe and wick moisture better.

Most jumpers opt for handmade leather boots, and when you gear up to jump, plastic ankle braces are Velcroed over the top for support on landing.

In terms of head protection, we've come a long way since the leather football helmets worn by the first generation of jumpers. There was a while in the late '60s when guys were wearing Bell motorcycle helmets like Evel Knievel, minus the stars and stripes.

Some jumpers still rock a classic Bell. Most wear high-end ski helmets now, though. Face guards are mandatory, and a sports mouthguard can help keep you from chomping off a chunk of tongue on a bad landing.

It's always a good idea to rinse off your mouthguard before

you pop it in, in case it accidentally fell down someone's pants when you weren't looking.

Some things are just not sacred around a bunch of savages.

We each carry a personal gear (PG) bag the size of a small backpack. Add Nomex flight gloves and accessories like a "Jack the Ripper" hook knife—perfect for slicing tangled shroud lines—and you're talking anywhere from seventy-five to ninety-five pounds of equipment.

As we say, ounces make pounds, and pounds equal pain. More weight means a harder landing and a tougher pack-out. At Kernville a lead crew member used to say "dirt hurts, dude" to remind us to clean every last bit of crap out of our packs from previous missions.

A sign on the NCSB loft wall says HIGH RENT DISTRICT. The message is clear: this is one place on the base you don't want to linger as a rookie. It's where most of the senior jumpers hang their gear.

The loft is also where all the parachute action happens. Packing a chute takes anywhere from forty-five minutes to an hour. First every parachute is hung in the loft and checked from apex (top) to risers (bottom) for any kind of wear or damage: rips in the fabric, frayed lines, burrs around the connector links.

Then you stretch the canopy and lines out on one of the long rigging tables. After checking the steering line and doing a four line check, the apex is tied off to the deployment bag (D-bag). Then you fold the canopy, in a series of steps, to fit it inside the D-bag. The lines are stowed in a zigzag pattern and the risers secured with break tape, to hold them in place for the first few seconds you're in the air.

The final step is "wrapping the present," putting everything inside the back tray that keeps it protected and ready for its one-way trip.

I had to pack twenty parachutes to be certified to pack my own. Each one had to be inspected by an FAA-certified senior rigger or master rigger. I'll never forget number 20. After the rigger looked it over, instead of placing it on the shelf, he put it on his own back.

"OK, let's go do a practice jump," he said. He couldn't have shown any more clearly how much you have to trust the person who packs your canopy.

ONE AFTERNOON THREE WEEKS after we passed rookie training, the fire call—an old air-raid siren—howled across the base.

People scrambled for their gear. This morning, for the first time, my name was on the jump list. The list dictates your position on the next plane and is updated daily. Whoever is at the top is jumper in charge (JIC), and every time you come back you start over at the bottom.

This morning all five of us rookies were on the list. This was our maiden fire jump.

We had already practiced suiting up over and over until we could do it in two minutes or less. Now we ran to the racks where our jumpsuits hung on wooden pegs to do it for real.

Not every base uses these quick suit-up racks—invented by jumpers, of course—but it definitely saves time, because you don't need someone else's help to get your suit on, like you do at some other bases.

I stuck my arms in the sleeves, then sat down and zipped up the legs. My pockets were stocked with essential gear, and a main chute was already attached to my back. All I had to do was zip up, close the harness, and pull a packed reserve chute off a hook.

I grabbed my helmet and gloves and went to the spotter for a top-to-bottom gear check (spotter check). After a thumbs-up, I hustled outside with everyone else toward the rising rumble of the plane's engines. We climbed on board and sat in our jump-list order.

"All on board, all aboard!" yelled a spotter as the last jumper stepped in.

The pilot and copilot had already done their preflight check. The plane rolled toward the runway, the pilot throttled up, and eight minutes after the siren sounded we were airborne.

YOU COULD ALMOST HEAR the buzz of nerves and anticipation. We talked a bit over the engines and wind, leaning in towards each other to be heard. I double-checked my equipment.

The plane headed due south. In the main cabin, the noise of the engines made conversation a bit sporadic.

Both spotters sat up front with the pilots. Even though they don't leave the plane, spotters play a critical role in the jump process. (They're all jumpers and rotate through the same jump list.)

A spotter's job is to coordinate with dispatch, the pilots, and the JIC—the first one out the door—to make sure everyone exits and lands safely. Spotters are an objective eye in a situation where adrenaline or testosterone can distort good judgment.

Jumpers trust them with their lives, so they have to stay cool no matter what.

When we were on station, somewhere east of Bend, Oregon, the main spotter came back to the main cabin.

The fire was already "going," meaning it had enough momentum to keep itself burning but wasn't huge yet. It was big enough that another load of jumpers from Redmond was already on the ground.

Two sets of streamers fluttered toward the jump spot the spotter had chosen. They took about a minute to hit the ground, which meant we should too.

The plane banked left on final approach, and the first stick stood up. To the uninformed they would have made a strange sight, waddling in their bulky tan jumpsuits, covered with straps and buckles and bulging pockets. The high collars, smooth helmets, and wire face masks made them look like insects. All that was missing was a pair of antennae.

But to us they looked like what they were: jumpers ready to do their job.

When my stick was up, I made sure to keep both hands over the red handle on the reserve pack on my chest. In the air, your reserve chute can save your life. But inside a plane with an open door, it's a loaded gun.

In 1973, a jumper named Gene Hobbs was working as a spotter for a load of NCSB jumpers on a DC-3 in Alaska. Longtime NCSB jumper Ash Court was his assistant spotter. Hobbs was reaching for a box of streamers when his emergency chute deployed by accident. In an instant the wind sucked the canopy out the open door. Seconds later it sucked Hobbs out too.

Unfortunately, he went out sideways. He smashed his head and shoulders against one side of the door frame and his legs against the other. After briefly snagging on the plane's tail, the chute carried him to the ground, unconscious.

Nobody could jump to help him because of the damage to the plane. The impact had peeled the fuselage back six inches around the doorway and torn the door almost completely off its hinges.

As the plane circled overhead radioing for help, another jumper's reserve chute popped open inside. His companions leaped on it before anything happened.

Rescuers found Hobbs covered with mosquitoes but alive. He had broken his neck and one leg and had no memory of what happened. He wasn't paralyzed, but he was left with nerve damage and double vision that ended his jump career.

I protected my reserve carefully as I stepped to the doorway, went through the checklist with the spotter, and made my exit.

The world outside the plane was bright and quiet. The sounds of the engines trailed away overhead, replaced by rushing air and the whump of the parachute opening.

Then the only noise was the creak of harness straps and the rustle of the canopy overhead as I steered toward the landing zone. It was big and open, and I could see the circles of other parachutes spread out below.

Everyone landed safely. When we had regrouped, one of the veteran jumpers came over and handed out baseball hats with the NCSB logo.

"*Now* you're rookie smokejumpers," he said.

THE FIRST ORDER OF business was a safety briefing. To make sure everyone is on the same page, wildland firefighters use what's called the LCES system. It's an acronym for Lookouts, Communications, Escape routes, and Safety zones—the four most important things you need to keep from getting burned.

Lookouts can be on the ground or in the air, depending on how remote the jumpers are. Any intelligence that lookouts gather about changing conditions or approaching hazards is conveyed to the firefighters, usually by radio. Sometimes the jump plane or another aircraft will relay communications between dispatch and crews on the ground.

In case things get too hot, you always want to have at least two escape routes to a safety zone. The fire line itself often works as an escape route, but having only one isn't enough. Conditions on the ground are constantly changing: flames shift and people move around, tire out, drift out of contact. No matter what, you always need a way to get to safety.

The LCES system is meant to defend against the unexpected. It only works if it's in place before you engage the fire and is constantly reevaluated as conditions change.

Next we collected the cargo boxes where each had touched down under its own small parachute. After all the jumpers are out, the spotters kick the cargo out at a lower altitude, dropping it precisely where the jumpers on the ground need it to be. (It was this special talent, among others, that brought many jumpers to Southeast Asia to work for the CIA during the Vietnam War.)

To a jumper, a cargo box is a UPS package from Santa Claus. These boxes hold everything we need to be self-sufficient for at least the first forty-eight hours on the fire line: hand tools, chain saws, first-aid kits, sleeping bags, cubies of water, food.

The menu includes campfire favorites like freeze-dried meals, energy bars, trail mix, candy, beef jerky, Ramen noodles, or anything that comes in a can: chili, meat, soup, fruit. Spam is highly prized. If there's no Spam, some jumpers can get a little pissed off.

Everyone has his or her favorites. You might be a Snickers dude or a canned peach guy. Some jumpers seem to like eating corn and oatmeal all day. Others bring extra food, like frozen gourmet meats shoved in a leg pocket.

I've never met anyone who really likes MREs.

When I jump on any fire, one of the first things I do is to grab my food and water and shove it in my pack. I've learned the hard way.

After a few times returning to the jump spot tired and hungry and finding that some professional eater has inhaled most of the food—including all the good stuff—you learn to take precautions. Food box poaching is no laughing matter.

At our base there are always two food boxes: one for you, one for your jump partner.

CANOPIES GATHERED, CARGO UNPACKED, LCES in place: it was time to fight the fire. Otherwise known as cutting line, our main job on the ground.

Just as every fire is different, so is every fire line. But there is an overall strategy. Picture a fire from above: it has a head, where the flames are spreading the fastest; usually a couple of flanks, or sides; and a heel, often back near the point of origin.

The idea is to start building line at the fire's heel, ideally from an anchor point like a road, a river, a lake, or a cliff. This should keep the fire from flanking you, that is, sneaking around from behind to make a much bigger problem. You want to contain the flanks and pinch the fire off at the head, like fingers snuffing out a match.

That's how it works on paper, anyway. Sometimes even in real life.

Roads, streams, and trails can make good natural fire lines, and we're happy to use them if they're in the right place. Usually we have to dig the line ourselves once the sawyers have done their work. From scrubby bushes to hundred-foot trees, if it's on the fire line, it's getting chopped by those howling orange Stihls.

A fire line is usually between one and three feet wide, depending on the situation and the crew. In national parks, crews try to make fire lines as narrow as possible to keep from scarring the landscape. Some hotshot crews are known for the almost machinelike neatness of their lines.

Jumpers are somewhere in between. You want to dig an effective line while conserving as much energy as possible, since you never know how long you're going to be out. We're not worried about tourists complaining about a ruined view, but we're also often working with less manpower.

Lines are measured in chains, a term left over from seventeenth-century English surveyors. One chain is sixty-six feet, so that makes eighty chains in a mile. (And ten chains in a furlong, for your next trivia showdown.)

Line-digging speed is mostly dictated by terrain and vegetation. In moderate brush, a Type 1 crew of eighteen or twenty hotshots should be able to dig six chains of line, about four hundred feet, in an hour.

For jumpers there are extra variables like how many bodies we have and whether we have chain saws or just hand saws. It's always heavy physical labor regardless.

Sometimes firefighters are cutting into thick mats of tangled roots, using their pulaskis to slice their way through. On a slope they might have to cut small trenches to catch embers from rolling downhill. We're always looking for hidden heat, slicing open smoldering stumps and searching for hotspots where the duff is smoking from buried heat.

OUR FIRST REAL SMOKEJUMPER fire sucked. There was lots of dead and down, a.k.a. fallen trees, so we were constantly tripping over trunks and branches. Sweat stung our eyes and trickled down our grimy faces. The chain saws never seemed to stop roaring.

We dug straight through the night, chasing down the glow of spot fires in the darkness, like kids catching fireflies and stomping them to death.

A crew of hotshots came in the next day to help out. We were out for a few days in all. When we got back to the base, we were finally allowed to wear shirts that said SMOKEJUMPER.

We were still rookies, though. You're not considered a "real" jumper, at least at NCSB, until you've stuck around at least four or five years. Even now I consider myself an "old rookie."

Between missions we trained and worked on projects like prescribed burns, cutting hazardous trees, fencing projects, and so on. During wilderness first-aid drills, some of the group would be assigned imaginary injuries, from heatstroke to broken bones. The others would have to figure out how to treat and transport the "victims" using only the gear we'd normally bring on a jump, like packs and cargo chutes.

Hillbilly and I spent a lot of time trying to scare the crap out of each other. At night we'd hide in the darkness and leap out screaming. I'd get him coming out of the mess hall, and he'd hide under my van and grab my ankles.

Once I spent an hour and a half waiting in his closet as he watched TV in the next room. I eventually fell asleep; after years in the fire service, you learn to grab a snooze anywhere you can. When he finally came in, I woke up and threw open the closet door with a yell.

He jumped a foot in the air. "What the hell!"

"Give me a hand, dude," I said. "My legs are asleep." He laughed even harder as he pulled me out.

The base emptied out in the off-season as jumpers went on vacation, back to school, or off to other jobs for four to six months. Some jumpers traveled back east to work as arborists or on prescribed fires.

I returned to Riverside County for a few winters and started driving my van down to Baja California, Mexico. The Bahía de Los Angeles became my second home in the winter.

Sometimes I'd take paying clients on guided trips spearfishing or dolphin watching. Other times I'd just windsurf, kitesurf, or freedive, living off the ocean for weeks at a time.

If I got in the water early enough, I could usually catch enough food for the day by early afternoon. Between my van and the ocean, I was pretty much set.

A MISSION DURING MY second season took me three thousand miles in the opposite direction. In July 2000, we were requested to work out of a satellite base near Galena, on the Yukon River in western Alaska. As a California boy, it sure seemed to me to be the middle of nowhere.

Galena had about five hundred residents, a big deserted World War II air base, and little else. It was only accessible by air or water. In the summer the midnight sun made it seem even more desolate and creepy.

We stayed there for weeks waiting for an assignment, with nothing to do beyond daily PT and chores. We played midnight volleyball and kept an eye out for moose and grizzlies on our runs. Guys were so bored they'd have skidding contests on rusty old bikes we found lying around.

I sometimes pedaled one through the empty streets, every-thing gray and quiet, half expecting someone to pop out in a sundress or Don Draper suit like an episode of *The Twilight Zone*. I was having trouble sleeping. In fact, I was going a little batshit with all the waiting and the endless flat light.

One afternoon I was sitting out in the rain when another jumper walked out. "Are you fucking okay, dude?" he asked.

"Yeah. Why?"

"Well, because you're sitting out here alone in the rain."

I came back down to Earth and went inside. Part of being a

smokejumper is dealing with the hard parts of personal stuff when you're in the middle of nowhere and thousands of miles away. No cell phones, no Internet back then. It put a strain on every personal connection we had.

At least we had a great cook assigned to us. I quickly made friends with him and started snagging extra late-night snacks. I was always starving at night.

I'd just smile when the others would ask where the hell I got the extra rations. *That's right, bitches,* I thought. My dad taught me well: scrap when you can.

FINALLY, ON THE FOURTH of July, a call came in: a growing fire was threatening a group of cabins around a lake. Out of an eight-jumper load, three of us were from NCSB. Even though two of us were still only second-year "snookies," that jump plane carried approximately one hundred years of firefighting experience on board.

It was a twin-prop Dornier 228-202, a faster ship than the ones we used at NCSB. It was also a small door exit. To get ready to jump, you put your left leg on a step outside the door with your right leg bent inside the plane, kneeling to fit through the small opening.

When I was in the door, I asked the spotter if they were planning on slowing down on final. I could hear my jump partner laughing his ass off over the engine. The spotter just looked at me cross-eyed and told me to put my foot on the step. It was like sticking your arm out the window of a car—a Formula One.

Compared to the Northwest, Alaskan jump sites are relatively flatter, covered with rolling tundra instead of boulders and big trees. There are hazards, sure, including plenty of water to land in and huge distances to cover if you find yourself stranded.

On that jump I had my first experience with another special Alaskan menace. At about five hundred feet I could see thick dark clouds hanging in the air. What was that haze? The second my boots touched the ground, I found out: mosquitoes. Billions of mosquitoes.

If you've never been to the Alaskan bush in the summer, you have no idea how bad mosquitoes can be. The state has thirty-five species, and most of them love the taste of people. They can make herds of migrating caribou change direction and send little kids to the hospital.

Between mid-June and late July, round-the-clock sunlight turns the endless acres of wetlands into ideal breeding grounds for the little bastards. (Actually the biting ones are all females, but who's counting.)

We were there smack in the middle of prime season. It's the closest I've ever come to experiencing a biblical plague. Mosquitoes were in our mouths, in our food. The tiniest piece of exposed skin became a mosquito mosh pit. (A scientist once recorded 435 bites on his arm in five minutes.) When they bit, the mosquitoes swelled up like tiny grapes, and when you wiped your arms clear, your hand would come away bloody.

According to native legend, long ago mosquitoes only used to bite animals. One day an old woman came home and found that every piece of food she had stored up for winter was gone. The mosquitoes had eaten everything: fish, caribou, even her seal oil.

In a fury she tore off her clothes and ran outside, shouting, "You mosquitoes have eaten all my food, so now you might as well eat me too!"

That's how they found out people have nice, smooth skin that's easy to pierce, and no tails to brush them away. Ever since then we've been their favorite prey.

Thanks a lot, lady.

Not surprisingly, the cabins were unoccupied. The only people there were a couple with a young girl and a dog who were living in a tent while they built a cabin of their own. Until flames came over the horizon, our job was to provide assistance to them, conduct structure protection, and keep track of the fire's progress by radio.

The couple, both artists, had left the Lower 48 to make their dream of living off the land in Alaska come true. They appeared to have plenty of financial resources but, to me, they seemed a little out of place up here. Everyone was covered in mosquito welts, and the father's boots were wrapped with duct tape.

One of the jumpers was born and raised in Alaska. She noticed the guy was building the cabin from instructions in a book and was using birch planks, a wood that rots quickly.

She didn't mince words. "So you only want to have it for a couple of years?" she said. "You have a dog, that's good. Do you have a gun? If you're spending the winter, you should really have a gun to protect your family."

We couldn't force them to give up their crazy plan, so we just helped them move logs and played with the girl. The jumper talked half seriously about checking in on them by plane, maybe dropping a care package.

MOSTLY WE JUST TRIED to avoid the mosquitoes. One of the worst times was when you had to answer the call of nature.

Some parts of the body are just not meant to be bitten by insects. My first reaction was to swat. Big mistake.

Smokejumpers are nothing if not resourceful, though, and Hillbilly soon came up with a makeshift solution. If you covered your body with a trash bag, with a hole cut for your head, you could (mostly) avoid being eaten alive while you did your business. And thus was born the potty poncho.

The only real way to escape was to go out on the water on a boat. Ten feet from shore and the mosquitoes vanished. It was the strangest thing.

There were a lot of late-night pike fishing excursions.

We were thrilled to find an outhouse at the far end of the lake. We made that our incident command post and nicknamed it "Club Med." It had a water view, all the facilities, and a million biting insects.

The stories you hear of people going crazy from Alaska's mosquitoes sound like tall tales, but who knows—another week at Club Med and I might have flipped out myself.

We spent six days by the lake and the fire never got close to the cabins. The experience taught me a different side of being a jumper. We can be animals when necessary, but on that bug-infested pond, we were public ambassadors more than anything.

That, and there are some things no training can ever prepare you for.

CHAPTER 9

THE RIDGELINE ABOVE ME in the Okanogan-Wenatchee
National Forest was glowing red. A hundred yards away,
tree-high flames soared skyward with a sound like telephone
poles snapping in a windstorm.

"Jumper F, Ramos, do you copy?"

The fire was blowing up, as we thought it might. Three
jumpers were stationed above me on the narrow ridgeline. It
was maybe fifty yards across at its widest, scattered with wind-
twisted trees, with steep drop-offs to either side in some sec-
tions.

Two had already radioed in that they were heading up the
ridge to the safety zone. But I couldn't get a reply from the one
closest to me.

I knew he was probably double-timing uphill and couldn't
hear me over the noise of the surging fire and aircraft overhead.
Too busy to pull out his radio.

Nevertheless, as JIC part of my job was making sure all personnel were accounted for.

I called him three or four more times.

No answer.

AS A FIREFIGHTER, UNDERSTANDING what fire does—and more important, being able to predict what it's going to do—is a matter of life and death.

Fire can burn uphill, downhill, and sideways. It can jump across canyons, outrun horses, and hide underground for months. It can flow like water in any direction and create its own weather, from thunderheads five miles high to flaming tornadoes that snap trees like celery.

People have been studying fire since the first caveman burned his fingers trying to cook a mammoth steak. We've had plenty of time to watch it, fight it, follow it, and examine its charred path. Now researchers dissect flames in labs using wind tunnels and high-speed cameras.

So what have we learned?

Let's start with the basics. Remember seventh-grade science: *Fire is a spontaneous chemical reaction that releases energy as light and heat.* When it's plant material burning, that energy came from the sun and was absorbed by a leaf. It was converted by photosynthesis into lignin and cellulose (among other things), the two most common organic molecules on earth.

You've heard of the "fire triangle": fuel, heat, and oxygen, the three things fire needs to burn. In this case lignin and cellulose are the fuel, regardless of whether the plant is alive or dead.

Air is 21 percent oxygen, so there's plenty of that.

The aftermath of the "Big Blowup"—Coeur d'Alene National Forest (Idaho), August 1910. This historic fire burned three million acres, took eighty-five lives, and forever changed America's attitude to forest fires—and wildland firefighting. *USFS*

Fighting fire in the early days. Then as now, they were lucky if they had a water source nearby. *USFS*

On the fire line, working the fire's edge. The goal was the same back then: take the fuel away from the fire, leaving it nothing to consume. *KD Swann*

Fred Patten, Recreation Guard at Meriwether Campground, inspects the remains of a flashlight used in the Mann Gulch fire of 1949. The cross next to him marks the spot where Leonard J. Piper, a smokejumper, lost his life in the fire. 1969, Helena National Forest. *Philip G. Schlamp*

Johnson Flying Service with jumpers preparing for a mission. *Phil Stanley*

Pioneer smokejumper Francis Lufkin in 1939. This was Lufkin's first plane ride and first jump, in the Chelan (now Okanogan-Wenatchee) National Forest, Washington. *HC King*

Smokejumper soon after leaving the plane with the pilot parachute completely distended and the thirty-five-foot canopy unfolding. June 1940, Lolo National Forest, Montana. *K.D. Swann*

Johnson checking Lufkin's jumpsuit. Today we use a remarkably similar jumpsuit, with careful attention to detail, high-end textiles, and padding. These guys were way ahead of their time. *USFS*

Entrance sign at the "Okanogan aerial project," now known as North Cascades Smokejumper Base. Okanogan National Forest, Washington, July 1957. *Donald B. Stickney*

Some of the protective gear we still wear today. Virgil "Bus" Derry in a jumpsuit that then included a back brace and leggings. In front of Stinson Reliant SR-10, 1939, Intercity Airport, Winthrop, Washington. *H.C. King*

Lufkin holding one of the tree branches broken off by Chet Derry, who mistook a moss-covered larch for a pine tree. His parachute collapsed but opened again and set him on the ground easily.

Ground training for smokejumpers. Payette National Forest, Idaho, July 10, 1952. *Lowell J. Farmer*

Smokejumping squadleader Bill Carver demonstrating to trainees the inverted "V" trough, for strengthening ankles. Lolo National Forest, 1952. *WE Steuerwald*

Men on the conditioning obstacle course with stockades (the "torture rack"), performing leg, back, and abdominal exercises. Lolo National Forest, 1952. *WE Steuerwald*

The let-down simulator. This unit teaches trainees how to safely rappel out of a tree or any other object they've managed to land in. You can see the NCSB loft in the background, still the same building that we use today. *USFS*

New trainees practicing on the "mock-uprisers" designed to teach the "planing" maneuver and strengthen arm and shoulder muscles, 1952, Lolo National Forest. *WE Steuerwald*

Early rations and gear. *KD Swann*

Group of jumpers with Frank Derry in the center, about to take off in a Ford Trimotor plane at Missoula Airport, Missoula, Montana, for practice jumps with static line. *KD Swann*

Smokejumpers become very proficient with sewing machines. *Phil Stanley*

The parachute loft, where we make and repair all our gear. This is the heart of the operation. *Phil Stanley*

Fred Brauer and Jack Nash in the assembly room at the smokejumpers loft. Missoula, Montana, 1951. *WE Steuerwald*

Outside the NCSB loft, all geared up and ready to go. *USFS*

Smokejumper equipment on display at the Society of American Foresters meeting, Farmington Flats, Utah, 1946. *Paul S. Bieler*

Jump partners fully geared up with all the tools needed for fire suppression, including pulaski and crosscut saw, circa 1945. *Phil Stanley*

Double stick: two jumpers in the door getting ready to head to work. Note the spotter on the floor next to the door. Lolo National Forest. *Maurice Vogel*

Smokejumpers parachuting into Glacier National Park, Montana. *Martin Onishuk*

Smokejumpers descending. *USFS*

Radioing in after landing. *Phil Stanley*

Parachute jumper Dick Tuttle near the top of a one-hundred-foot lodge pole pine snag, waiting for assistance from then–Forest Guard Francis Lufkin. *David P. Goodwin*

Some of the early parachutes were made out of silk. In the rear you can see the Derry brothers' steering slots that made the Derry slotted parachute more controllable for tight jump spots. *USFS*

Then all you need is some heat. Any kind of spark will do: lightning, volcanoes, a person's cigarette. Heat drives flammable gases out of the fuel, which combine with the oxygen in the air and start to burn.

This process creates more heat, which forces out more flammable gases, which combust. Pretty soon you have a nice little flame going, plus a flying mix of burned particles and gases called smoke.

To stop the cycle, just remove any of the corners of the triangle. Contain it with a fire line so it uses up all its fuel and dies of starvation. Smother it with dirt to cut off its oxygen.

Water is good because it smothers and cools at the same time. The fire retardant or "slurry" that air tankers drop has additives like ammonium phosphate to make the water extra "sticky," fertilizers to kick-start regrowth, and red dye to show where it landed. Hopefully not on a firefighter's head, since a gallon weighs over eight pounds and a plane can dump thousands at a time.

That's what fire is. How about what it does?

There are three main things that affect how a wildfire burns: fuels, terrain, and the weather. We can only control one of those. Fuels can be anything from dry pine needles on the forest floor to three-hundred-foot redwoods. Light fuels like grass, leaves, and brush burn fast and hot, which is why you start a campfire with the smallest kindling.

Living plants that have lots of flammable resins or oils in their leaves, like sagebrush and Gambel oak, make excellent light fuels. When you have a dry landscape covered by these, like the chaparral of Southern California, look out.

Heavy fuels—trees, large shrubs, fallen logs, stumps, piles of logging debris—don't ignite as easily. But once they do, they're much harder to put out.

The next most important measurement is moisture content. The drier a fuel is, the better it burns. And smaller fuels dry out faster, since they have a higher surface-area-to-volume (SAV) ratio.

Put those together and you get the four fuel size classes, differentiated by how long their moisture content takes to equalize with the surrounding air. The fuel classes range from "one-hour fuels" a quarter inch in diameter or less, like grasses, to "thousand-hour fuels"—big fuels three to eight inches in diameter and buried deep in the duff of the forest floor, like dead logs covered in years of pine needles and leaves.

Under the right conditions, living green plants can ignite too. I've seen piñon pines go up like they were soaked in gasoline, lodgepoles shoot off in sequence along a ridgeline like Roman candles on the Fourth of July.

After baking in the sun all day, a hillside of Gambel oak or juniper can become saturated with invisible flammable gases called terpenes, just waiting for a spark to explode, a phenomenon called superheating.

More things to consider: How much fuel is available (the fuel load), and how is it arranged? Are flammable materials spread out evenly or clumped together? Is there more on the ground or up in the canopy?

Don't forget underground: smoldering tree roots, buried logs, ash pits, and coals can lurk out of sight from one year to the next, even under snow. Mop-ups often involve "potato patching," endless shallow digging with pulaskis for buried heat sources. Firefighters have to feel for heat with their bare hands.

Ladder fuels carry fire from the ground up into the canopy, where it's an order of magnitude harder to fight. Canopy fires sometime take off in a completely different direction from the ground fire that lit them.

Subalpine fir is a bitch in this regard. The same features that make fir trees popular as Christmas trees—densely needled branches that reach almost to the ground—also make them perfect ladders for flames.

Makes you wonder about people's sanity when they used to decorate trees with lit candles around the holidays, doesn't it?

I WAS DOING MY best to stay levelheaded as I called the jumper on the radio.

Jumpers don't need to be micromanaged. He knew what he was doing.

All I could do was take a breath and chill out.

It was mid-July 2013, an early fire for the Okanogan. This was turning out to be a big lightning year for the Northwest. Before the snow started falling, over a quarter of a million strikes would be recorded, double the annual record and four times the average.

Sometimes you get a load of guys you've worked with for years, and sometimes you get a load you've never worked with before. They're all highly trained, but it can be challenging as the JIC if you aren't familiar with each jumper's strong points and hangups.

This load was half and half. And it was shaping up to be a hard mission. We were on our own on the ground for the first few days, even though I had requested more resources and jumpers.

On top of everything, I had such a bad cough I felt like I was going to break a rib. At one point I coughed so hard my nose bled. (Later I found out whooping cough had recently made a run through the Methow Valley.)

More crew and supplies were due to come in at any time by helicopter. Earlier I had sent two jumpers to the helispot to manage the incoming support.

The other four of us started working above the fire. I gave the other three their assignments—two sawyers, one lookout—then hiked a few hundred yards down the ridge. I found an open rocky area that would work as a command post: satphone reception, good visibility of the fire and jumpers, everything a JIC needs.

I spread out my pack, satellite phone, solar charger, and assorted paperwork. There was some weather inbound—things were starting to kick up already—and with that kind of intel you want to have a heads-up. Our lookout had an excellent vantage point on the ridgeline. If necessary he could handle a large amount of the information and direction on the fire, especially if I got bogged down in radio communications.

This ridge had already burned through once on this fire, but there was still plenty of fuel left up high in the trees.

Sure enough, the wind started picking up late in the afternoon. Soon it was gusting over 30 mph. The fire surged, and it was time to head to safety. But where was the other jumper?

It wasn't more than a few seconds before his voice finally came over the radio, although it felt like longer. He had reached the safety zone.

"Roger that," I said, relieved.

Then I felt heat pricking my face. The wind had grown so strong that it was now pushing the flames *down* the ridge toward me.

It was now just a few yards away.

DOWNHILL OF A FIRE is usually the best place to be. But not always.

In general, flames tend to grow and speed up as they go uphill. Compared to flat ground, a fire will spread twice as fast on a 30 percent slope and four times as fast on a 55 percent slope. A downslope of about 15 percent gives the slowest spread; anything steeper and burning fuels falling and rolling downhill start to increase the speed again.

Terrain can affect fire behavior as much as fuels. At least you know the topography isn't going to change over the course of a fire season, a mission, or even an afternoon, which makes its effect easier to predict.

Along with the steepness of a slope, it's also important to consider the direction the slope is facing. In the Northern Hemisphere, slopes with southern exposure get more sun. Fuels tend to be lighter and drier—that is, more flammable— than on north-facing slopes. Once a fire gets going in a north slope's denser fuels, though, it can be more difficult to put out.

Put more than one slope together—say, in a canyon—and

things get interesting fast. River gorges and other kinds of deep ravines can make fires do all kinds of strange things. They change airflow in unpredictable ways, transfer heat and flying embers from one slope to another, and create microclimates, small areas of unpredictable fire behavior.

Narrow canyons, especially dead-end box canyons, can funnel winds like a chimney. Hot air rises up and flows out of the upper end and is replaced by more air pulled in at the bottom. If there's a fire, this cycle can fan the flames and turn the whole thing into a giant blazing wind tunnel.

Weather is the most fickle of the three main things that affect fire behavior. It's the only one that can change completely in the time it takes to eat a hamburger.

Wildland firefighters obsess over the weather more than your average meteorologist, and for good reason. For most people, the worst consequence of missing the daily weather report is getting a little damp on the way to work or having a less-than-perfect weekend at the beach.

For a jumper, hotshot, or anyone else on a fire line, an accurate forecast can mean the difference between living and dying.

Temperature and humidity are both important too; fires burn faster the hotter it is and often "lie down" at night when it's cooler and more humid.

But as I witnessed on the ridgetop, wind is the one feature you have to watch out for on an hourly or even minute-by-minute basis. Wind feeds fire with more oxygen and carries burning embers to light new spot fires. It preheats and dries out fuels, then pushes flames toward them.

Since sun-warmed air rises, winds generally blow upslope

during the day, peaking in the midafternoon and slowing or even reversing at night.

Not always, though. As a teenager in Southern California, I had seen what the Santa Anas, bone-dry downhill winds up to 60 mph, could do to a daytime blaze. I've seen gusts blow down power lines and roll a giant culvert across open fields, real Wizard of Oz–type stuff.

Thunderstorms are a mixed blessing. They can spark wildfires with lightning, fan them up with wind, and put them out with rain.

As storm cells grow and mature, they often create updrafts and downdrafts of 50 mph or more that can act like bellows on a fire.

Sometimes a storm cell just collapses and dumps rain. Other times, if a fire is large enough, it can create its own weather. Anvil-topped clouds rise into the stratosphere. These can act just like normal storm cells, complete with wind and lightning and precipitation.

At ground level, if conditions are right, the wind and heat and flames can start to reinforce one another in a hellish feedback loop called a firestorm.

In a firestorm, nothing is safe: sand turns to glass, metal runs like water, wood and human beings vanish into ash. Blazing tornadoes of flames suck up smoke and debris.

"Fire devils" are actually fairly common in intense wildfires. The smallest ones are only a few feet across with winds of a few dozen miles per hour. Large ones go down in history alongside names like Dresden and Hiroshima. The bombing of Hamburg during World War II created a thousand-foot-high fire tornado with 150 mph winds that tossed people into the air like so many leaves.

Natural firestorms can be just as bad. In the summer of 1871, the Upper Midwest was baked by drought and hot weather. Cold fronts are notorious for bringing sudden shifts in weather, and on October 8 one pushed across most of Wisconsin and Upper Michigan. The winds it brought fanned countless small fires into one massive firestorm called the Peshtigo Fire.

Survivors described a wall of flame a mile high and five miles wide that traveled faster than a speeding locomotive. Winds tossed train cars and houses through the air. People leaped into rivers and lakes to escape and drowned or died of hypothermia instead. Desperate parents cut their own children's throats instead of letting the flames take them.

In the end, 1.2 million acres burned and between fifteen hundred and twenty-five hundred people died. The numbers are fuzzy because so many town records were destroyed and so many bodies were burned beyond recognition or simply vaporized. The Peshtigo Fire is still the deadliest fire in U.S. history.

So why does hardly anyone know about it today? Probably because of a more famous fire that happened on the same day. About 250 miles south, the Great Chicago Fire destroyed a good chunk of the city's downtown and killed about three hundred people.

Fuels, terrain, and weather interact in countless ways when it comes to fire. Mountains create thunderclouds. Drought makes fuels more flammable. Steep slopes have the same effect as high winds. Damp fuels offset high temperatures. And so on.

Nothing illustrates how the complex equation can turn deadly better than the Storm King fire in the summer of 1994.

CHAPTER 10

O N JULY 2, 1994, lightning sparked a small blaze on Storm King Mountain near Glenwood Springs, Colorado. It smoldered for three days, within sight of the Colorado River and I-70, before anyone was dispatched to fight it.

By July 6, the South Canyon Fire covered about 125 acres on a steep west-facing slope below Hell's Gate Ridge. (It—the fire, not the ridge—was named, mistakenly, after a canyon on the other side of the river, but is better known as Storm King.)

Sixteen jumpers were brought in, along with a helitack crew, including Rich Tyler, and twenty hotshots from Prineville, Oregon. A total of forty-nine firefighters eventually joined forces.

After they landed, the firefighters cleared two helispots on the ridge above the fire. They divided into groups and started digging two fire lines, one along the ridge and a smaller one heading down the slope of the west drainage to flank the fire. The helispots were designated as safety zones, as was the bottom of the west drainage, a deep gulch choked with dead and down trees.

It was an ugly fire from the start, on a steep hillside in dense piñon pine and scrubby Gambel oak baked by drought. The brush grew taller and thicker as they worked downhill.

Some of the crew reported later—and said at the time—that the whole situation gave them a bad feeling. Digging line downhill, in bad terrain, during the hottest part of the day, in the hottest part of the year.

Any one of these alone could be fine; together, in hindsight, they're a checklist of red flags. The firefighters might also have been sensing, somewhere below conscious thought, the faint odor of terpenes in the air as the hillside vegetation superheated.

Don Mackey, a jumper from Missoula who was JIC and directing the effort, said more than once, "There's nothing on this hill worth getting killed over." Still they kept working. That was just the culture at the time: you did your job and kept concerns to yourself unless they were head-slappingly obvious.

At 4 P.M. a cold front moved in. A "red flag" weather warning had been issued earlier, but it never reached the people on the ground. Strong winds followed the interstate up the river gorge and then turned north up the west drainage below the firefighters.

A small ridge blocked their view of the growing fire, but there was little sense of urgency at first. It was only when the full flame front came into view that they realized how bad the situation was.

As boaters floated under blue skies down the Colorado River and residents of Glenwood Springs videotaped the smoke rising far above, firefighters on the slopes below Storm King started running uphill for their lives.

They found themselves trying to outrace a crown fire. Parts of the hillside had already been burned through down low. Now flames were racing through the tops of the tall shrubs without touching the ground.

The firefighters divided into two groups. One bunch of smokejumpers, under Mackey's direction, headed straight up what became known as Lunchspot Ridge at the southern end of the fire line.

They expected Mackey to join them and bring up the end of the line. Instead, he turned around and raced back down the trail heading for the other group, including more jumpers and the Prineville Hotshots, as they were retreating back up to the ridge along the line they had built that morning, moving parallel to and above the fire. Mackey wanted to "clear the line" to make sure everyone made it out safely.

The trail grew steeper as it approached the ridge. People stumbled, abandoned tools, started passing each other. The wall of flames covered a quarter mile in two minutes at close to 20 mph, fast enough to catch birds in midair.

The flames soared nearly 200 feet above the ridgetop when they reached the crest. An NCSB jumper named Eric Hipke reached the top about five seconds before the flame front. He grabbed the back of his neck hoping for some tiny bit of protection. A blast of superheated air lifted him off his feet and then knocked him down like a fist.

His screams were probably the only thing that kept his airways from being seared closed.

With badly burned hands, he managed to scramble across into the east drainage on the other side of the ridge.

No one behind him survived.

Out of twenty-two shelter deployments on the fire there were twelve casualties, including Mackey, nine hotshots, and two McCall jumpers, Roger Roth and Jim Thrash.

Rich Tyler and another helitack crew member named Robert Browning Jr. made it farther away starting from the top of the ridge at a helicopter landing spot, but were trapped by a deep gully at the head of the west drainage. Their bodies weren't recovered for two days.

The whole thing took seven minutes from start to finish.

The survivors stumbled down the east canyon, the side away from the fire, trying to raise their friends on the radio. They arrived at the highway and within half an hour the fire followed them, and that drainage was burned out too.

Storm King hit the wildland firefighting world like a bomb. The three jumpers were the first to die from fire since Mann Gulch, forty-five years before. (Three others had been killed in jump operations, and nine others on fire missions—seven plane crashes, one helicopter crash, one drowning.)

The circumstances were disturbingly similar: steep canyons, uphill escape routes, strong winds that caused unexpected but predictable fire behavior.

Ironically, just a year before, Norman Maclean's classic *Young Men and Fire* had made Mann Gulch the firefighting equivalent of a household name.

Storm King was also the first time more than one female wildland firefighter was killed. Women made up six of the forty-nine crew members but four of the fourteen casualties. Wildland firefighting is a relatively small world, and losing people you know is part of the job. Sometimes you just don't come home. Everyone handles it in their own way. For me, I try to honor them and all the others who have fallen by doing everything I can do to educate others, improve our gear, and work to get it into more firefighters' hands.

As any JIC does on difficult missions, I have debated with myself whether to dig in and request more resources or pull back and minimize the risk to the crew. It can be a hard call. Bad choices are almost always clear in hindsight.

The crews on Storm King were in a precarious situation. Digging fire line downhill is an aggressive approach, and as a result it's a trade-off. The work goes faster, but your clearest escape route, the fire line itself, runs uphill.

The main cause of the disaster was clearly the extreme weather event. If the crews on the ground had had any warning, they would have pulled out long before the blowup happened.

The official fire investigation turned into a predictable clusterfuck of politics and finger-pointing. Two of the investigators refused to sign the final report.

Storm King did lead to some improvements in safety and communications, at least. Getting weather forecasts to firefighters in the field was made a top priority, and every jumper was issued a radio. Firefighters were trained to deploy shelters on the run, not just standing still, and research into better fire shelters began in earnest.

Crews also felt more comfortable questioning or even refusing orders they felt were too risky. This used to be a sure way to get yourself labeled chickenshit. Now more and more firefighters were willing to put the brakes on. In the decade after the tragedy, fatalities for Forest Service firefighters fell by over 40 percent.

Storm King was a wake-up call. It made people think hard about what it's worth risking to fight a fire that doesn't directly threaten any lives. Those of us with structural firefighting experience were already familiar with that mind-set. If there aren't any lives in danger it's not worth putting your ass on the line.

BACK ON THAT GLOWING red ridgeline in the Okanogan-Wenatchee National Forest, with the fire cutting off my escape route uphill, it was starting to look like my ass might be suddenly on the line.

I grabbed my radio. "All rotors on 242, I need you on my location ASAP."

We had two helicopters doing bucket operations on the fire, dumping water on the flames with pinpoint accuracy from a few hundred feet up. Right now they were both dropping water on the ridge so the fire didn't jump over to the leeward side.

From a distance, their precise aerial maneuvers looked like a conga line with only two dancers. As soon as one emptied its water bucket, it flew off to refill as the other made its drop. We were lucky to have a dip site (a refill spot) close by, so that part of the dance only took a few minutes.

"IC 242, your location?" came the reply from above.

I told the pilot where I was. In a few seconds, he was hovering overhead. I told him I needed a recon from his viewpoint.

"You need to get to the high point on the ridge top," he said. That wasn't reassuring. Helo pilots are all business, so when one gives a straight-up move-your-ass directive, you better listen.

There was only one way I was going in that direction. The rotors paved my path, keeping the ridgeline in check with multiple bucket drops.

I alternated between cursing and grim chuckles as I hustled past the flames, close enough in places to toast marshmallows. Worst-case scenario I could jump in a water bucket and get a ride out. It's been done before.

Usually you only see this kind of downhill burn in places with extreme winds, like the Santa Anas in California. It showed how when things are aligned right you can get extreme fire behavior in a place that doesn't usually produce it—like the Northwest.

It took a few minutes to make the safety spot, an open area with little fuel to burn. It's funny how your mind works. Most of the way up I was thinking how I'd never hear the end of it back at the base.

WE WERE ALL BACK up on the burned-over ridge the next day. The support I had requested had finally arrived in the form of another load of jumpers.

"How's it going, PR?" said one jumper I knew. Depending on who you asked, the nickname stood for Puerto Rican or public relations, since I do a lot of base tours and other kinds of outreach. "Having fun babysitting this shitty fire?"

"What do you think, dude?" I was happy to have the experienced help. After yesterday's adventure on top of sleepless nights of coughing, though, I wasn't in the best of moods.

His noticed a blackened blob of metal on the ground. "What the hell?"

We had landed with an extra chainsaw, and a sawyer had cached it for use as a backup if necessary. We do this with extra gear all the time.

Then the fire made its run.

Aluminum melts at 1221°F. This blackened lump was proof of just how high the temperature had been right where we were standing.

A few feet away sat a load of plastic water blivets, seventy-two gallons long-lined down by rotor.

They were completely untouched.

CHAPTER 11

R OCK!"
The yell came from upslope, followed by a crashing
noise in the trees.

We were on a fire near Lake Chelan, a long, narrow mountain lake southwest of Winthrop. It's one of the prettiest places
in the North Cascades, surrounded by steep forested hillsides
and snow-capped peaks to the west.

I always looked forward to missions here because demob
(demobilization, a.k.a. heading home) usually meant a boat ride
out and a good meal at the landing.

At the moment I was mopping up the lower left flank of the
fire alone. The other three jumpers were uphill.

Earlier that morning they had called down that there were
some big boulders up above that could start rolling.

There had already been a few warning shouts, though nothing too serious—one more day on the job.

Just in case, I picked out a big fir tree nearby, about five feet
in diameter, to hide behind.

The crashing grew louder. Whatever it was, it sounded big. *This should be cool,* I thought.

I looked up and saw a boulder the size of a golf cart rolling downhill, flattening everything in its path.

It was heading straight for me.

THERE MAY BE OTHER jobs that are more dangerous, statistically, than wildland firefighting. But needless to say, jumping is still a world away from sitting behind a desk. You're working in an inherently dangerous, unpredictable setting. A fire environment has multiple layers of hazards that are constantly changing and interacting.

As with most activities, one of the most dangerous parts of fighting fire is simply getting to the scene. Vehicle crashes, including plane and helicopter accidents, are the most common cause of fatalities outside of fire itself. Cardiac events like heart attacks are next.

If you're lucky, the worst part of the plane ride is getting airsick. The Sherpa is especially bad in this respect. That plane is just a horse, with its head-piercing engine noise and the way it feels like it's always circling just a little bit.

One flight took us through five states in a single day. The plane came from Oregon, picked us up in Washington, then we hit Idaho, the California border, Nevada, and, finally, Oregon again. At least three times we had to stop to refuel. A few jumpers were puking their guts out toward the end. The visuals and smells nearly started an all-out puke fest for the rest of us. I managed to hold down my lunch, but just barely.

We were nearing the pilots' eight-hour flight limit (not to mention ours) when they found a fire for us somewhere in Oregon. The sun was low in the sky—we can jump up to half an hour after sunset—when we landed in a meadow.

One guy had joked on the plane how he never got airsick. By the time he landed, he was so green he just released his parachute and lay down as darkness fell. He didn't get up until later that night.

The fire was small enough that those of us who weren't still too sick could handle it.

We were fine with that. Picking up the slack when necessary is part of the job.

EVEN THOUGH WE USE what is probably the safest parachute system ever developed, in the end we're still jumping out of planes.

Bad landings have left jumpers with twisted or broken ankles, shattered femurs, wrenched knees, dislocated shoulders, fractured vertebrae, and concussions. They don't call it "rough terrain jumping" because it sounds cool.

Regardless of how much you train, some landings are going to hurt no matter what. One of my worst happened just a few minutes' flight time from NCSB.

It was my fifth year on the job. My assignment was to monitor a fire we were watching under a let-burn directive. After landing I was to take pictures and notes on the weather and send the intel back to base.

The jump spot was a small patch of green with some rocky spots that summer jumpers call scabs. I was second in the stick.

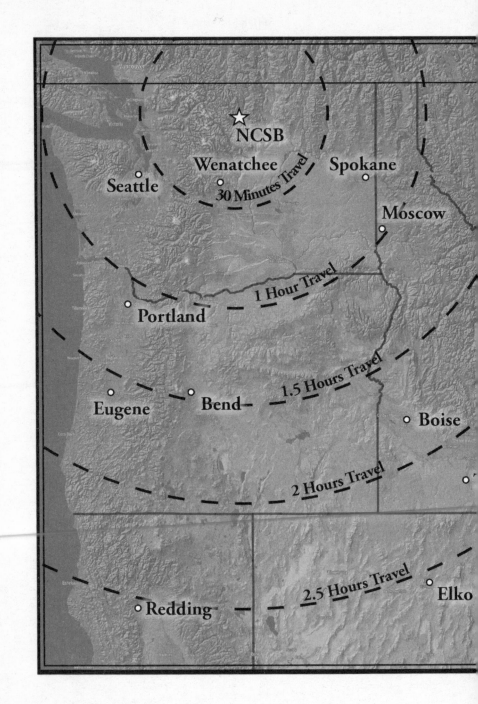

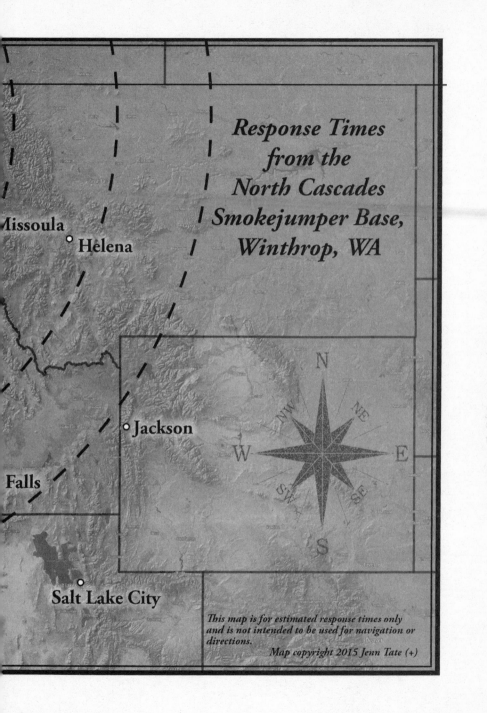

**Response Times
from the
North Cascades
Smokejumper Base,
Winthrop, WA**

Missoula

° Helena

° Jackson

Falls

° Salt Lake City

N

NW   NE

W   E

SW   SE

S

*This map is for estimated response times only
and is not intended to be used for navigation or
directions.*

Map copyright 2015 Jenn Tate (+)

At one hundred feet I knew I wasn't going to hit the happy zone like my jump partner had. He was already on the ground yelling encouragement: "Keep it tight, keep it tight!"

This one was going to hurt.

At least I landed into the wind, so my forward speed was as low as possible. Some jumpers joke you can land in concertina wire if the wind is in your face.

None of that here, but it was a stony minefield. Even though I had a soft touchdown, a textbook PLF was not happening.

In this kind of situation, anything you leave sticking out—like, say, an arm—can snap off like a chicken wing. All you can do is keep it tight and do your best imitation of a bowling ball.

I tucked as small as I could and rolled. There was crunching. At some point my left hand smashed against a rock. *Great,* I thought—*there goes another finger.*

"Are you OK?" my partner yelled when I didn't hop up with my usual speed.

"I'm fucking fine, just give me a minute!"

I picked myself up slowly, waiting for the warm sensation of flowing blood. I pulled off my glove to survey the damage. What do you know: all five digits, present and accounted for. I was bruised to hell, but not even bleeding.

Even better, the whole cooked chicken I was carrying in my leg pocket was still intact. So was the roll of spicy marinated mozzarella next to it. We stuffed our faces that afternoon.

JUMPERS DON'T DWELL ON getting hurt. In this job, a high pain threshold is considered an advantage. In that way it's like being a professional athlete, minus the million-dollar salaries and the world-class physical therapists.

For better or worse, complaining about being sore or tired is a sure way to end up ostracized.

In the late 1970s, some NCSB jumpers were working a fire in the Glacier Peak Wilderness Area in the North Cascades. It was a long mission, so they had extra supplies dropped in.

When it was over, they were looking at a nine-mile pack-out through steep country. Contrary to standard procedure, they decided to burn some of their trash, seal it in a bag, and bury it instead of carry it out.

A wilderness ranger found out and dug the trash up. He was understandably pissed. The base manager agreed to come in to talk to him, hopefully placate him a little.

It was an early-morning jump into a high basin at fifty-five hundred feet. The jump spot was windy and long shadows made it hard to judge altitude. The senior jumper hit a downdraft near the ground and smoked in from two hundred feet.

He caught a rock high on his right leg, shattering the femur into five or six pieces "like a bowl of jelly," he said later.

They had to evacuate him by helo. Doctors put his leg back together like a puzzle, sawing an inch and a half block of bone in the middle of his femur into four quadrants, 90 degrees apart, positioning them with a titanium rod and plastic bands, and then leaving the fragments to calcify where the bones were joined together. He spent eleven weeks on his back and thirteen weeks on crutches.

While an accident like that might motivate some people to reconsider careers, this guy was spotting, ground-pounding, and rappelling the next season, and then jumping again after only a year off jump status. His right leg was now an inch and a half shorter.

A few years later, to prevent future orthopedic problems, he went to a hospital in Seattle where doctors had developed a new procedure. They removed a piece of bone from his good leg and sewed it back up, knowing the muscles would shorten themselves naturally.

Five weeks later he was jogging again, back to normal except for one thing. When he left the plane over Glacier Peak he was six feet tall, and now he was five feet ten. He made another two hundred and thirty jumps before he retired.

A water landing sounds simple, but it's not always a pleasant experience. Once I landed near the edge of a lake near Mount Baker in Washington. With the reflection off the surface I couldn't tell exactly how deep it was.

You know how sometimes you're walking down the stairs and you think there's one more step but there isn't? My landing was like that.

My feet hit the bottom a tiny bit sooner than I expected. The shock caught me off guard and my teeth snapped shut, clipping off a piece of the side of my tongue. (Pro tip: shut your mouth before you hit the ground.)

I talked a little funny for a day or two, and I wore a mouth guard for a few years after that.

I also found some tadpoles in my leg pocket.

Jump in the Cascades long enough and chances are you'll end

up hanging in a tree at least once. I've done it about a dozen times.

A tree landing means a lot of extra work, so you try to avoid it if you can. And usually the smaller the tree, the better.

If a tree landing is your best (or least bad) option, you want to cap the tree well.

That means lining up the top between your legs like gun sights, pulling the brakes and, hopefully, if you had enough time to do everything right, spreading the canopy over the top of the tree like a hat.

If you end up well hung, so to speak, your canopy will make a solid rappel anchor to get to the ground.

Paying attention as you drop your letdown line could save you hours of grief, and luck helps too. A good toss will give you a clean rappel line. But if you aren't paying attention in a wolfy tree that's full of crap, and toss your rope, you'll have a terrible time getting down. In that case it's best not to throw it at all, but reroute it back to your leg pocket as you rappel down.

If you don't cap a tree cleanly, it can be a nightmare. You might end up hung on a limb, in which case you better hug that tree like a cat and start thinking about dumping gear to lighten up.

A canopy can snag on branches and deflate. The next thing you know the jumper is bouncing down between the branches like a Plinko chip on *The Price Is Right,* grabbing at anything to slow down.

A bad tree landing is a sobering thing to see, like a very unfunny cartoon explosion with stuff flying everywhere. Our jumpsuits are tough but sharp branches can still punch through, or even impale you.

If you hear the sound of snapping branches, you can't help but give a silent prayer, hold your breath, and listen for anything—cursing, usually—as proof of life.

You never leave a chute hung up even if it's completely shredded. It's not just littering the forest; each canopy represents close to $2,000 of taxpayers' money.

If you can climb the tree and pull it down, great. Otherwise you're looking at cutting off the treetop, or maybe even the whole thing.

It might have to wait until you're finished with the fire, but eventually that canopy has to come down.

On the ground we have to deal with the usual hazards of working in the outdoors: dehydration, headaches, sunburn, poison ivy, wasp nests, snakes, and wild animals.

The list gets a lot longer when you add the risks of fire and the tools we use to fight it.

Year after year breathing smoke and ash can cause chronic respiratory issues, not to mention black snot. Chain saws cut through legs as easily as branches.

Sawyers are supposed to cut trees and shrubs flush with the ground. If they don't, sharp little stumps called stobs are left behind, sticking out of the ground like punji sticks. God help you if you fall on one of these. I've heard tales of these ending up where the sun doesn't shine. That would suck.

Wildland firefighters also must keep an eye on their pee: if it's brown and they've been working especially hard, it could be a sign of rhabdomyolysis, a buildup of electrolytes and muscle proteins in the blood that can permanently damage the kidneys.

That's one reason we have a rule of thumb of drinking a gallon of water per day during arduous duty.

One of the biggest dangers on a fire are falling snags. You never know when or where a dead tree or limb is going to fall. The big ones can be as thick as you are tall.

A normal-looking tree may be rotten or burned through just under the surface. A falling trunk covered with branch stumps might as well be studded with swords.

Snags are called widow-makers for good reason. Dead trees and branches have killed plenty of firefighters, including a jumper out of Redding in 2013. Helmets help, but they could be better. That's why I helped a leading company design a better helmet in my off-duty time.

If we're required to wear head protection, I want something that actually works.

Rolling stones—not the band—are surprisingly common, to nonfirefighters at least.

Intense heat causes everything to expand, loosen, and crumble, including soil and stones. Flames burn away roots that hold rocks in place. Gravity takes over and things start heading downhill.

Runaway rocks are common enough that firefighters have given them a tasteful nickname: "Bowling for Hotshots."

ON THE LAKE CHELAN fire, the boulder heading toward me was plowing aside trees like a bouncing bulldozer. I could feel the vibration through my boots.

I've rolled some rocks in my time, mostly as a kid in California. Once my dad and I aimed a big one at an old VW bug someone had abandoned in a ditch. It hit the car hard enough to spin it halfway around.

This one was much bigger.

I did my best Indiana Jones impression and lunged toward the fir tree. Just as I reached it the boulder slammed into the other side in an explosion of debris. The shock felt like the roll-over car accident I had in my twenties.

I opened my eyes and saw the boulder hurtling away below me, heading at a slightly different angle, blazing a clear, splintered route all the way down the hill, as far as I could see.

I yelled to one of the other jumpers to come down and be my witness. He found me standing beside the tree staring at a huge chunk of bark almost as large as me that was lying on the ground.

We both knew that if the tree hadn't been there, he would have been picking me up in pieces.

I ended up following the nice, clean path cleared for me by the boulder down to the nearest trail, then hiking out to the rendezvous spot for a helo pickup.

I never did get that damn boat ride.

EVERY NOW AND THEN you'll get a mission that's just a checklist of misery.

On one such occasion, I and another NCSB jumper started out with a good landing on a small lightning fire north of the base.

Our cargo boxes, on the other hand, ended up hung in the trees.

The whole point of smokejumping is to get to the fire as quickly as possible. You can't screw around once you hit the ground. If there were more than just us two, we could leave someone behind to retrieve the gear. But there wasn't.

We had no choice but to leave almost all our firefighting tools, food, water, and cold weather gear dangling in the branches and head off to find the fire.

I had only one canteen of water on me, which was frozen. That and some Gatorade mix and a Snickers bar.

Then it got worse. The forests of the Pacific Northwest have the densest biomass in the country—sometimes lots of huge trees, but in this case, an incredibly dense understory.

This fire was burning somewhere in that brushy tangle. To find it we had to get on our hands and knees and squirm through tunnels of vegetation like some kind of jungle commandos.

The fire was hardly smoking at all, which meant it was a bitch to find. Over the radio, air attack snidely suggested I try and sniff it out. I'm notorious at the base for having an almost uncanny sense of smell; if I even get a drop of milk on my clothes, it will drive me nuts. I laughed at the transmission, suggesting they come down and give me a hand.

No luck here, though. After a brief but intensely frustrating search, we finally found the smoldering pig, dug some line around it, and got it confined for the night.

We made it back to the jump spot by sunset. We were parched, but it was too dark to get the cargo down now. We had to wait until sunrise.

We shared a few "Gato shots," two capfuls of water mixed with a little Gatorade.

Not a good idea.

I didn't know it at the time, but ingesting too much glucose and too little water can cause bloating and diarrhea. (Now I know; and I carry a better electrolyte replacement mix on every jump.) I don't think I've ever been so thirsty, even in triple-digit Southern California summers.

The temperature was dropping fast, but our sleeping bags were somewhere overhead in the darkness.

We both had the same idea simultaneously: out came the fire shelters. They're designed to keep heat out, but turns out they're pretty good at keeping it in too.

We deployed the shelters and settled in for the night. I ended up getting a great night's sleep—the silver lining, so to speak, to a shitty day. I'm still not sure why this isn't standard training in case of emergency.

The next day we got everything down from the trees. Then it was time to head back to the fire and put it out.

We were down to one cubie of water—a cardboard box with a five-gallon plastic bladder inside. Normally these are for drinking, but under some circumstances—such as this—we use them to help put out a fire.

Anything to get out of this shithole faster.

We drank up, filled our water bottles, and saved the rest for the fire.

Back into the jungle tunnels we went.

Usually you carry a cubie by sticking your pulaski through the little cargo strap on top and slinging it over your shoulder.

Here, of course, that was impossible, crawling through dense thickets on our hands and knees.

Just to move on this hellacious hillside I had to put the strap around my wrist. The box kept twisting and banging into me until I was ready to cut it loose and watch it tumble away.

But we needed the water, so all I could do was thrash around and practice my French.

When we reached the fire, we were able to put it out quickly. You'd be amazed what five gallons of water and two pulaskis can do.

Even then we weren't done yet. The local forest helo reconned us a pickup spot and estimated it was an easy hike away.

From the air, distances can look completely different from how they are on the ground. I had a superintendent back in California who was fond of saying, "Just one more chain, Snapper." This always meant we'd be walking to China.

I could hear his voice in my head as we hiked and hiked and hiked some more.

Hours later, we finally reached the helispot and called for pickup.

JUMPERS ARE ALWAYS LOOKING for new and better gear to make their lives easier. Aside from a government-issue helmet, fire shelter, and a few other basic necessities, we have to buy everything ourselves.

The list doesn't even include boots, a firefighting essential, although rumors are in the air that we might be getting a stipend for those.

After that night in a shelter, I did some research and discovered a camping hammock made by Hennessy Hammock.

I picked one up and found it to be one of the finest inventions ever made for sleeping in the backcountry.

Since then I've never jumped without one in my PG bag. I've only had to sleep on the ground twice more: once because there were no trees, and once because I was just too damn tired to set it up.

My "office view" from the ridgeline fire in the Okanogan/Wenatchee National Forest, North Cascades. To a jumper, these mountains are always beautiful—and sometimes pure hell, too.

If these wings could talk. This impressive artwork watches over the daily operations at NCSB. It is made out of two pulaskis and dozens of jumpers' gloves collected throughout the years.

Examining a reserve parachute in the NCSB loft. As a jumper you're always checking and re-checking your gear to make sure everything is in top condition and ready to go.

Packed chutes ready for service in the NCSB loft, with retired parachute harnesses hanging above. There are years of history on these walls.

Jump 9 on standby at NCSB with a Redmond jump ship in the background. The smoke column in the distance is from one of the lightning-sparked fires that would eventually join with others and grow into the Carlton Complex of 2014.

Some of the specialized gear I jump with. The gear each jumper carries can vary depending on training and expertise.

Suited up at sunset at NCSB, checking out some new gear for the next mission.

A nighttime lightning strike: smokejumpers have a saying, "We jump at dawn," that pertains to moments like this.

Jumpers away! The Casa 212 drops a load of jumpers over the Methow Valley near NCSB. *Rick Stewart*

That's me coming in on final approach to the jump spot. *Rick Stewart*

We work to stay proficient, typically jumping every seven to fourteen days depending on fire activity. *Rick Stewart*

Down safe and ready to work. Our jumpsuit is padded from head to toe and can sometimes weigh more than seventy-five pounds with gear. *Rick Stewart*

Bring it in, hump it out. Pack-outs are one of the hardest parts of jumping. This was an interesting one at Crater Lake, Oregon—turned out to be 154.8 pounds.

Fire 242: this 2013 ridgeline fire in the North Cascades is starting to wake up and make a push down canyon.

In the middle of a six-day mission on steep and rugged terrain near Leavenworth, Washington. On this one I used high-end solar gear so we didn't have to depend on helicopter support for batteries.

A 2012 late season fire in Washington. We pulled out the next day when it grew too large. Mother Nature put this one out.

The view from a plane coming on station over an established fire. Large fires can create their own weather, including rain, hail, high winds, and lightning. *Doug Houston*

A lightning-caused fire in Washington State in late September 2012. This was taken during our morning briefing on a road below, where I was going through the day's work assignments as task force leader trainee.

My first experience with the sheer power of a large fire: the view from the roof of our house in Wildomar, California, in 1987.

The Wildomar fire was practically in my backyard. Southern California is famous for its extreme fire behavior.

Tanker dropping fire retardant in Washington State. *Bill Moody*

Sometimes my house travels with me. Here on a taskforce assignment in Washington, the Sportsmobile makes a great response and command vehicle—not to mention a home.

One of the reasons we do what we do: protecting natural resources like this giant cedar in Washington State.

Ceviche time in Baja California. Keeping in shape throughout the year is key, so in the off-season I often freedive up to fours hours a day, eat healthy, and take plenty of naps.

Patience pays off: a good day with good wind and no other windsurfers to worry about. Baja California.

Catch of the day: the bounty from the ocean with respect to our harvest. Baja California.

Guests are welcome at NCSB, the birthplace of smokejumping in 1939. Come by for a tour of the base—the best time is in the summer—and we'll start at this historic sign.

CHAPTER 12

THE BACK WALL OF the NCSB loft is decorated with memorabilia and a few photos. One of the pictures shows a jumper stooped under a huge pack that towers above his head. He looks like some kind of medieval peasant carrying a load of goods to market.

Guess who that is?

The setting was Crater Lake National Park. Redmond is the closest jumper base, so the park is usually their territory. But just as jumpers from other bases get to see our backyard in the Cascades, I've been lucky enough to jump there a few times.

The deep, almost alien blue of the lake and the jagged rim of the collapsed volcanic caldera make for some world-class scenery.

The park is huge, though, much bigger than just the lake. On this two-man mission we jumped into a part called the pumice desert, a barren area covered in powdered rock and ash from the same eruption that created the lake seventy-seven hundred years ago.

I was out one morning answering the call of nature when I heard an elk bugling nearby. I couldn't see anything—we were in the densely forested side of the park—but I had never heard one this close.

I started sneaking toward the sound through the woods. I wanted to see this thing. I kept searching quietly through the trees and bushes until finally, stepping around a trunk, I almost stumbled into a bull with a large rack off to my left. He gave an angry grunt and charged.

Let's just say if I hadn't done my business already I would have shit myself. There was nothing to hide behind and no time to run, so I stood my ground.

He passed within a few yards and went crashing off into the trees.

When my heartbeat returned to normal, I looked around the dense forest and realized I was a bit turned around.

Did I mention I was JIC?

As I realized I was turned around, I knew I needed to pay close attention and retrace my way back to camp. Without a radio or a compass, I had to rely on my experience and landmarks to work my way back. It took a bit, especially if you include my elk excursion and sightseeing. Once I knew I was finally getting close, I hooted a few times in case the other jumper could hear it. He was only a rookie on the fire and probably thought I was hurt or something. At one point I had even heard a plane that sounded like a jump ship and thought, *Shit, my radio's back at camp, I'm the JIC, and they are trying to contact me. Just great.*

It was a good lesson in how you should never go off, even

a few yards into the woods, without your radio and a compass in your pocket.

When I finally got back to camp, it turned out nobody was looking for me or worried about my extended absence.

"Did you hear me hoot a few times?" I asked the rookie.

"Oh yeah," he said. "I thought that was some hiker!"

WE FINALLY FINISHED WITH that fire and returned to the jump spot to pack up to leave.

Normally any cargo that burns goes into the campfire to lighten the pack-out. Here, however, we were within sight of a scenic viewing area. Visitors might be watching, and you can bet the rangers were. We had to carry everything out.

As I shouldered my pack I heard a few stitches pop in the shoulder straps. Luckily the hike was flat, with only scattered soft spots and holes from ground varmints to watch out for. I spent most of it struggling to stay upright.

My jump partner obligingly took a picture.

It took us about two hours to go about two miles. When we reached the truck I backed up to the tailgate, leaned back, and unclicked my strap buckles with a sigh of relief. That feeling of sudden weightlessness never gets old.

A tourist had drifted over and started peppering me with questions.

"Sir, give me a second," I said, hands on knees, trying to catch my breath. It took a few seconds of stretching before I could straighten my spine out all the way.

When we returned to base, my jump partner tried to convince me to let him weigh our packs. I figured it would be a serious morale breaker if it only came in at 110 pounds. I told him, "No, dude, I'm okay."

A few minutes later I heard some ruckus in the cargo area and voices saying my name. Great, I thought. My pack usually was under 110 pounds—I must be turning into a pansy.

When I entered the room, one jumper said, "Holy shit, dude, you had 154.8!"

I looked at the scale. He was right.

It was my heaviest load ever for me. My pride felt a little better. The popped stitches made sense.

Soon a new photo joined the others on the wall: a not-too-tall jumper bent under a backpack heavier than him.

AS YOU MAY HAVE assumed, there's a certain protocol to fighting fire in national parks. Firefighters need special approval for things like retardant drops, cutting down trees, and using motorized equipment like chain saws and pumps. We're often restricted to light hand tactics, essentially nineteenth-century firefighting technology. The technical term is MIST tactics—Minimum Impact Suppression Techniques.

The whole experience can be a bureaucratic nightmare.

On another Crater Lake mission, a local fire chief called on the radio as soon as we landed. "You guys are not here," he said.

"Can you please repeat?" I said.

"You're not even here. Do not dig holes, don't disturb anything. Don't even fart."

I laughed to myself, but after a glance around I got the picture. We were in some kind of special research area that was pristine even by park standards.

Where we were standing had the cleanest forest floor I've even seen. It looked like some millionaire's property where a caretaker used a Miele vacuum on it every few days.

A PACK-OUT ISN'T A race. Everyone travels at his or her own pace, usually alone.

You've been busting ass for days, working in the dirt, and sleeping on the ground. You're lucky if you have only 110 pounds on your back.

You're free to stop for a dip in a river or some huckleberry grazing, anything you want, as long as you make it to the pickup spot on time.

Sometimes you get lucky and find a good trail—even a game trail—that makes for an easy hike out. ("Easy" being relative, of course.)

That doesn't happen often in the North Cascades, though. So the pack-out is often the hardest part of a mission—and sometimes it can take twice as long as you anticipated it would.

Once I was on a two-manner with another jumper from NCSB, on a small ridgeline in the Cascades. It was early summer, with plenty of snow lingering in the mid to high country.

We put the fire out without any problem. When it was time to pack out, we radioed one of the ships flying overhead for intel on the nearest road.

The helitack on board gave us some coordinates. "There's

one about a quarter mile below you," he said. "A couple hours at most."

I looked at the steep slopes all around us. There were deep patches of snow in every shady spot and on most north-facing slopes.

I shook my head. Two hours my ass. Yet another piece of helicopter intel that was certain to be a bit different on foot.

We shouldered our packs and headed out. "It's gonna take us at least four hours," I said.

Sure enough, the route that looked so short and easy from the air was anything but.

No trail, for starters. Our route took us across one particular north-facing slope that was steep and covered with snow. A man-sized cheese grater of jagged boulders waited at the bottom. If a guy tripped, he'd better get that pack off quick before he started sliding.

I tried to think Jedi thoughts and float across the surface crust without breaking through. My jump partner was heavier and was soon postholing knee deep.

"Hey, dude, think light!" I stopped to watch and laugh as he floundered. I wasn't far behind, but I figured I could stay on top of the crust.

I started to punch through about halfway across. In some spots I went in past my knees.

Now it was his turn to laugh. I heard him yelling something from above me but I was too focused on getting across to listen.

When I stopped for a breather, he said, "Look down to your right."

A shallow trough ran down through the snow to the rocks

below like a poorly planned sled run. There were deep grooves on both sides and traces of dark wiry hair in the middle.

It was the unmistakable ass track of a sliding bear.

The grooves must be where it tried to use its claws to slow down, like a mountaineer self-arresting with an ice ax.

It looked like Smokey was having some fun, but I wonder how banged up he got at the bottom. In any case, I'm glad I wasn't around. That would have been one pissed-off carnivore.

"Son of a bitch, don't fall now," I muttered.

We crossed the snowfield without incident and kept going. That two-hour hike took more than four hours.

Near the end, I ended up having to grab thick hanging vines to cross a slippery creek: Tarzan of the Pacific Northwest.

ANIMALS ARE SMART—THEY DON'T tend to stick around when there's a fire nearby. It's rare to see a charred carcass. We do occasionally cross paths, though.

On one Kernville helitack mission we were hunkering in for the night near a small creek. We didn't carry tents and usually weren't allowed to make fires, since our supt believed sleeping on the ground built character. Being a California boy, I hate being cold, but orders were orders.

After dark we heard a commotion near the creek. We grabbed a headlamp, and by its light we saw a big black bear playing in the water. He was jumping off the bank like a diving board, swimming back, and doing it again. It looked like he was having a blast.

He didn't seem to mind we were there, but we decided the

situation warranted a fire. Just in case. We piled enough pine-cones to last the night and slept warm as our friend splashed in the darkness.

Later that night, the local forest lookout tower called on the radio asking us about a new start in the area we were in.

"We have a large bear in the area," was our radio transmission reply.

IN THE DOWNTIME AFTER a fire is out, some of us go looking for dinner. Lots of jumpers are skilled hunters and fishermen; in another life they would have probably been mountain men.

Once many years ago, on a full load mission in the Okanogan, in the Pasayten Wilderness near the Canadian border, I set out into the woods with my trusty slingshot.

One of the jumpers who was on the mission saw me heading out. "Where are you going?" he said, half joking. "You city boys can't hunt!"

Later that evening I was back at camp with enough for dinner, grouse cleaned and ready to eat. All by slingshot.

We ate like kings that night.

IN THIS PROFESSION JUMPERS have to find the humor in the midst of the days that really suck. Otherwise they won't last long.

There's a plant called devil's club, a relative of Siberian ginseng that thrives in the Pacific Northwest forests.

Native cultures use it for all kinds of medicinal treatments. If you try to hike through it, however, you'll learn why its scientific name is *Oplopanax horridus*. It's covered with brittle spines that break off under your skin and are almost impossible to get out.

I got to know this evil shrub intimately on the west slope of the Cascades in Washington. It was the end of a fire mission. I and another NCSB jumper volunteered to recon a way out while the rest of our crew stayed behind to mop up.

We left early in the morning carrying just our PG bags, maybe twenty-five to thirty pounds each. It was only five or six miles to the nearest road.

As we were packing up, an NCSB rookie had told us he thought the path was impassable. We both laid into him immediately. "You're a jumper now, rookie! What the hell do you mean, impassable?"

Within a few hours we weren't so cocky. The broken terrain was making our compass act funny, and the vegetation was so thick we couldn't get a GPS signal. Most of it was devil's club.

We flailed through thickets for hours, tripping and falling, our faces and backs stinging with thorns.

At one point I got so frustrated I bit a branch. That just left me with thorns in my mouth.

We followed a river as much as possible to escape the plants. After being tormented by their barbs, I welcomed the freezing water and slippery rocks. More than once I just lay down in the water and floated a few yards, exhausted. I could only drift a little way each time from all the rocks and debris.

There was no way the jumpers back at the fire could catch up and make it out in one day. My jump partner radioed the JIC to tell him, in so many words, we'd hiked into hell and they should call for a helo pickup.

All we could do was keep thrashing. At one point I had to stop to scarf down a can of beanie weenies. As I finished my lunch, I saw a lone wood duck surfing a wake in the river, the only other living thing I had seen for hours besides a giant slug.

Wonderful, I thought. *Now I'm hallucinating.*

The others must have taken our advice, because impatient calls started coming over the radio hours later. They were at the pickup spot and wanted to go home—where the hell were we?

As dusk began to fall, I started looking for a hooch site to dig in for the night. Just then my partner's voice came on the radio: "I'm at the fucking trailhead. You're almost there dude, just keep heading downstream."

An hour later I heard a hooting through the trees, some-thing we do to give each other a bearing when we're close. It was one of the other jumpers who had gotten a helo ride out. He had hiked in a little ways to help guide us out, and now he was a little disoriented.

I couldn't help laughing. "Now you know what I did all day, dude."

The JIC hiked in as well so we could leave this Club Med. Together the four of us reached the pickup spot as the sun was setting, almost fourteen hours after we had set out that morning.

We spent the night at a local ranger station. Whoever had slept in the bed last had used nice shampoo, because the pil-low smelled great. I relaxed and enjoyed the luxurious smell of a woman's freshly washed hair . . . as I drifted off to sleep, it occurred to me that I really did hope it was a woman's pillow and not some guy with long hair who liked good-smelling shampoo.

BAD LANDINGS, ROLLING ROCKS, and shitty pack-outs are all occasional hazards. The biggest danger on a fire, of course, is fire itself.

Almost half of all recorded fatalities on wildfires in the United States have been caused by burns or burnovers, when firefighters can't get out of the path of a moving flame front.

A burnover is a disaster regardless of whether it ends with people dying. It means someone screwed up badly or was really unlucky—often both.

Every firefighter carries a personal fire shelter as a last resort. The idea goes back at least a few centuries. In 1804, William Clark and Meriwether Lewis were trekking across North Dakota when they came across the aftermath of a fatal prairie fire. With his typical creative spelling, Clark wrote in his journal: "A boy half white was saved unhurt in the midst of the flaim . . . The course of his being Saved was a Green buffalow Skin was thrown over him by his mother . . . the Fire did not burn under the Skin leaveing the grass round the boy."

Modern fire shelter development began in the late 1950s by the Australians. The shelters were bell-shaped, made out of aluminum foil laminated to fiberglass cloth, and looked like a teepee. The firefighter would stand inside. Later in the '60s the U.S. began experimenting with little silver A-frame pup tents.

A shelter is supposed to reflect the heat of a fire and trap enough cool, breathable air to survive a burnover. I've never had an occasion to test this in person, and I pray I never do.

The hottest part of a wildfire is around two-thirds of the flame height, around 2,600 to 2,800 degrees. At ground level, the temperatures are at their coolest but can still be as high as 1,800 degrees. A person can survive 200 degrees, maybe even 300 for a short time.

Then just a few breaths of superheated air can make your throat spasm closed and your lungs start to fill with fluid. Most fire deaths are from suffocation, not burns.

The Forest Service made shelters mandatory in 1977, the year after three hotshots died and one was badly burned in a fire near Grand Junction, Colorado. The firefighters had left their shelters behind in base camp and probably would have survived if they had them.

First-generation shelters weren't any good at withstanding direct flames or extreme temperatures. When flames touched them, the foil would quickly start to delaminate the adhevsive at around 450 degrees, and after that they were useless.

Out of 1,239 documented deployments since 1977, the Forest Service says fire shelters have saved 321 lives and prevented 390 serious injuries.

At the same time, forty-one firefighters died after fully or partly deploying their shelters. Some didn't get inside in time; others left too early or couldn't hold on in the flaming hurricane of a burnover.

The rest died because their shelters failed them.

There's no excuse for a piece of safety equipment not doing what it was designed to do—every time.

In the 1990s, after decades of calls for better shelters, the Forest Service ordered the Missoula Technology and Development Center (MTDC), its main fire research center, to find a better design. The shelters had to work better but they also couldn't be too heavy, and they couldn't cost more than $75 each.

The government eventually settled on a design with a flattened oval shape like an overstuffed sleeping bag. The M-2002 New Generation fire shelter is made of separate layers of woven silica and fiberglass, with foil laminated to the inside and outside. It weighs over a pound more than the old one and packs larger, and also comes in a size large for tall people.

Almost all firefighters were using the new shelters by the end of the decade. They're better than the old ones, but they're still nowhere near good enough. The adhesive that holds the aluminum foil to the cloth starts to break down and disintegrate at around 600 degrees. (At least manufacturers have stopped using the cyanide-based adhesive.)

A shelter needs to work in every situation, from grass fires to timber crown fires. It should be able to survive a two-thousand-degree burnover, because those do happen.

Would you drive a car if the seat belt only worked at less than 40 mph?

A shelter that doesn't do what it's supposed to offers a false sense of security, encourages more risky behavior, and raises the overall chance of accidents. That's why firefighters in Canada and Australia don't even carry them. It's also the reason I'm strongly supporting the development of a new fire shelter, which we'll get into later.

The best way to avoid problems with a fire shelter is to

never have to use it. If you're a firefighter with no choice, the deployment process has stayed the same.

First you find the best location possible, ideally an open area free of burnable material. If you have time, cut away the closest fuels and toss aside flammable things like chain saws, gas cans, and fusees we use for starting fires.

Pull the shelter from its plastic carrying case and shake it open. ("Shake and bake," as they say.)

Pull it over your back from feet to head like a fitted sheet. Then lie facedown on the ground. That's where the air is coolest and most smoke-free. Bring some water and a radio inside if you can.

Hold the floor of the shelter against the ground as tightly as possible. Heat and smoke and toxic gases will come through any gap.

Then hold on for dear life. Fire winds can be strong enough to toss you in the air. The violence and heat and noise of a burnover can make even veterans panic.

Firefighters have been killed after leaving their shelters too soon. Did they think their odds were better trying to outrun the fire? Or did they just want to get the inevitable over with quickly?

Who knows. Deploying a shelter is a psychological effort as much as a physical one. If you have to do it, you know one of two things is about to happen: you're going to live or you're going to die.

CHAPTER 13

W E WERE EATING DINNER in the mess hall on July 10, 2001, when the news started coming in about missing fire-fighters just north of the base.

The NCSB mess hall can be a loud place, filled with jumpers and anybody who happens to be at a fire camp nearby—pilots, hotshots, helitack, engine crews—shooting the shit and telling (and retelling) old stories and jokes.

It was another hot and busy summer in the North Cascades. Severe drought conditions had primed the area for wildfires, with temperatures in the high 90s and relative humidity in the single digits.

The day before, the hot exhaust pipe of a DNR fire patrol truck had sparked an explosive fire in tall, dry grass about twenty miles south. In its first twenty-four hours, the Libby South Fire had grown to over one thousand acres and forced an overnight evacuation of the entire Libby Creek watershed.

Now maybe three dozen people were enjoying the company and the famously tasty chow when radios around the room started filling with ominous chatter. I closed my eyes for a second. News like this is never welcome. But if you're in the fire service long enough, it's guaranteed to happen at some point.

Most experienced jumpers don't skip a beat at reports of injuries or fatalities. We've learned the long, hard way that you can't do much after the fact, and that often the best thing you can do to help is to focus on the job at hand.

I finished my food; something told me we were going to get involved, and I didn't know when the next real meal might be.

After dinner a call came over the PA: three other jumpers and I were to report to the office as soon as possible. As we walked over we could see the unmistakable sign of a blowup to the north: two massive thunderheads with a quiver of lenticular clouds like flying saucers between them. It looked like an atomic bomb had just gone off near the Canadian border. It was a sure sign of high winds aloft and extreme fire behavior down below.

"We have confirmed shelter deployments up north along the Chewuch," the base manager said when we reached the office. The narrow, winding river canyon was about thirty miles north of Winthrop. "I need four jumpers to head up there and look for possible civilian survivors. You guys good to go?"

The radio chatter at dinner was already a bad sign. If that kind of talk makes it onto the airwaves, that means bad shit has already gone down. Now a shelter deployment, which probably meant a burnover. Nothing good.

It was a genuine request for volunteers, not an order. The immediate aftermath of a large fire is a dangerous place. But if people might still need help, there was no way we were going to say no.

We packed four chain saws and gear into a van, and a few minutes later were rolling out the gate into the long evening shadows.

The rugged walls of the Chewuch River canyon formed a steep V that rose almost three thousand feet on both sides. There was just enough room at the bottom for the meandering river, a narrow belt of trees and thick brush, and a dirt road on the west side of the canyon.

The road dead-ended at a popular trailhead at the canyon's northern end, not far from the Canadian border. The heavily forested gorge was full of dead and down timber, a perfect bed for fire, with a thick understory of shrubs and bushes.

In 1929, the Remmel Fire burned forty thousand acres in the Chewuch River watershed. In 1994, it came close to burning again when the 4,780-acre Thunder Mountain Fire dipped into the canyon.

The Thirtymile Fire, the one we were headed out to help with, was named after a nearby peak. It had started the day before from a carelessly abandoned picnic fire in the upper canyon. The previous evening, when it was only a few acres, a full crew of hotshots was sent in on initial attack and worked on it through the night. During the night, a twenty-one-person fire crew from the Okanogan-Wenatchee National Forest called up for the Libby South Fire was redirected to help with the Thirtymile Fire instead.

Even when it's this close to a base, jumpers aren't called for every fire. Remember there are fewer than 500 of us on duty

most years, and in the height of the summer fire season, jumpers are often reserved for starts in places with no road access.

THE NORTHWEST REGULARS #6, as the second crew was called,
had rolled up the Chewuch canyon in two vans around 9 A.M.
They joined the hotshots and two engines that were already
there.

The Regulars were a Type 2 crew made up of firefighters
from two different Forest Service ranger districts, Naches and
Leavenworth. Many of them had multiple seasons of wildfire
experience, but they had never worked together as a group.
Eight were rookies, the youngest eighteen years old. Ellreese
Daniels, the forty-seven-year-old IC, was the third choice for
the position after fire managers couldn't track down two others
higher on the list.

At first it seemed the crews would be able to have the fire
under control by the end of the day. Only a half-dozen or so
acres were burning on the east side of the canyon, across the
river from the road.

The Regulars split into three squads and sent a lookout up
on a rocky outcrop. The canyon was so deep that radio signals
could only go up, so a small lookout plane circled overhead to
relay communications to dispatch. If worst came to worst, the
pilot could direct the crews to safety zones.

The road, mostly one lane, was the only escape route. One
way in, one way out: one of nature's warning signs.

When the Regulars started digging line around 11 A.M., one
problem followed another. Four of their pulaskis broke. They

couldn't get their two pumps to work consistently, so they couldn't pull water from the river and douse the fire as they had planned.

A helicopter with a water bucket was delayed for hours, in part because of confusion over whether it was allowed to scoop water from a stream that held endangered fish species.

As the temperatures climbed toward 100 degrees, flames started to spread through the "dog hair" thickets of underbrush faster than the crews could control them. Flying embers lit spot fires on the east slope and the narrow strip between the river and the road. Bone-dry trees started candling, exploding into flame like briquettes soaked in lighter fluid.

The Regulars had been up most of the night traveling and their energy was ebbing. Flames were eating through their hoses and spotting across the fire line.

By midafternoon they decided the fire was beyond control. It was time to back off, regroup, stay safe. So they did, at least at first.

The lookout was ordered down, and everyone gathered on the road to rest and eat lunch. The crew watched as what was now a full-blown crown fire spread from treetop to treetop. By now the blaze covered a hundred acres. It was an awe-inspiring sight, one many of them had never seen before.

With the flames moving away from them and on the other side of the river, they felt safe enough to relax, sharpen tools, and take pictures. Some even snoozed. While they were resting, an engine drove past heading up the canyon.

After a short break, a call came from the engine crew. They were still fighting a few spot fires about a quarter mile up the canyon. Could the Regulars send some people up to help?

Maybe the presence of the engine gave a false sense of security. Maybe the Regulars' crew bosses thought they could just keep driving up the canyon if they had to escape; apparently some of the crew didn't even know the road dead-ended, since their maps only showed the part of the canyon where they were working.

In any case, even though the crew was tired and the fire had already been written off as a lost cause, fourteen crew members, including Daniels, headed up to help. Some drove up in one van, and the rest were dropped off by the other, which then left.

Within minutes it was clear they had made a mistake. The fire was spreading fast and was now large enough to form its own thunderhead—those clouds we had seen from Winthrop. The smoky air was almost too hot to breathe and rising winds were lighting spot fires on both sides of the road.

The engine drove back down the road to the lunch spot and safety, followed by the remaining six Regulars in the second van. The flames were so close to the road they had to shield their faces from the heat as they drove past.

Up the road, the radio came alive with warnings. Flames were visibly closing in on that narrow escape route. Daniels and the rest needed to get the hell out of there, right now.

The Regulars started back down toward the lunch spot, four on foot and ten in the van. They found a wall of tree-high flames blocking the way. The fire had spread across the bottom of the canyon and was eating its way up toward them.

They were cut off.

Everyone piled into the single van. They turned around and drove back up the road to find a safety zone.

About a mile farther up the road, the river made a wide

bend around a sandbar and the canyon widened. A large rock slide spilled down the west slope almost to the road. The air attack plane on station confirmed the river bend was the most open place in the upper canyon.

Burning branches and pinecones rained on the van's roof as the Regulars parked at the rock slide and climbed out. Tensions were high, but this place seemed green and peaceful compared to what they had left behind.

Given the situation, it was the best place they could be. They were stuck but safe, in radio contact with command and the eye-in-the-sky overhead. The main flame front was out of sight around a bend. Even if the fire came this far, it would surely pass around them.

As all firefighters have done at times, they stopped and watched the fire. Some lit cigarettes. Others took pictures of the pillar of smoke, white on top and furious orange at the bottom. One scribbled frantically in his journal, describing the growing wind and the growl of the fire.

According to the official report, this is where the breakdown in leadership began.

To everyone's amazement, a Dodge pickup appeared on the road from the upper canyon. Bruce and Paula Hagemeyer had driven past the fire crews earlier in the day on their way to the campground two miles up. A pair of hotshot supervisors had scouted up the road earlier to make sure no one was left, but somehow they had missed each other.

The Hagemeyers had been relaxing, oblivious to the danger, until the thickening smoke convinced them it was time to pack up.

Now they found themselves trapped with the firefighters, with no protective gear or emergency training.

Six Regulars walked a short way up the scree slope for a better view. Just a few yards up from the road, they could see smoke filling the bottom of the canyon and rising in two huge columns that crept closer and closer. The air grew dark with smoke, and the sun turned blood red. The rain of embers turned into a blizzard of ash and fist-sized fireballs.

When the fire appeared around the bend, they could see it had spread across both the river and the road to the west side of the canyon.

Instead of passing by, it was roaring toward them with a noise like an oncoming freight train.

They could hardly hear themselves as they shouted at one another to deploy their shelters. At 5:24 P.M., eight small silver domes appeared on the road. Both the Hagemeyers crammed in one shelter alongside crew member Rebecca Welch.

The six on the scree slope sprinted higher in a futile attempt to find a better place to deploy. They scrambled into their shelters in a tight cluster one hundred feet above the road as flames fell on them like a tsunami.

WE TURNED UP THE Thirtymile road about forty minutes after leaving the base. It didn't take long on the winding gravel road to reach the deployment site.

The survivors were already gone. The charred remains of the Hagemeyers' pickup truck sat on its rims, its camper shell melted into aluminum slag. The Regulars' van right next to it looked completely untouched.

We could see the remains of fire shelters glinting along the road, in the river, and up on the rocks. The corners of some of those on the rocks were peeled back, revealing glimpses of the bodies beneath. A firefighter with a backpack pump was dousing the nearest one with great care.

We stopped and climbed out to prep our saws with oil and gas. One of the others drove, while I took a position by the side door, and the other two sat in the back with the doors open.

Our destination was the end of the road, where the chances of finding any surviving civilians would be highest. But from here on up it was going to be hard going. Dozens of burned trees had fallen across the road, and more were falling constantly. We'd have to cut our way through every one.

We reached our first charred trunk in less than a minute. All of us but the driver jumped out and started sawing as fast as we could. Rocks and small boulders were scattered around the road. When the chain saws quieted, we could hear the crack of trees toppling and the thump of fire-loosened rocks bouncing downhill.

It seemed like it was just a matter of time before something big and heavy came crashing down on the van, or one of us. It was enough to make you shrivel in your shorts. (Farther down the road, a falling tree hit a truck carrying the Okanogan County sheriff, the county coroner, and a few deputies; it knocked off a bumper but caused no serious injuries.)

Our progress was frustratingly slow. Sometimes the fallen trunks were only a few feet apart. It was good we brought four chain saws, because two of them ended up going tango union (a.k.a. tits up) and stopped working. Murphy's law seldom disappoints: if anything can go wrong, it will, usually at the worst possible time.

It was late evening by the time we reached the end of the road, about two miles from the deployment site as the crow flies. Three civilian vehicles sat gutted by flames, and the air was thick with lingering smoke. A Forest Service law enforcement officer had followed us to help with the search.

There's a surreal kind of calm after a fire goes through. The wind and noise and blinding light are gone, leaving behind a silent, blackened moonscape.

The sun had disappeared over the rim of the canyon, but there was still a faint glow to the west. Small spot fires and embers flickered in the dimming light. It was a trip through hell's backyard, everything either burned black or glowing.

We parked the van where the road ended at a turnaround. A small, primitive campground and trailhead were on the other side of the river. The bridge across was still on fire.

We ran across fast enough to keep from getting burned. "Anyone here?" we yelled. "Hello?"

The only response was the hiss and pop of dying embers. It was no place to linger. We made a quick search, called for another minute, and then ran back across the bridge to the van.

We had to clear just as many trees on the way out of the canyon as we did on the way in. Working by the glow of headlights, we cut through another labyrinth of downed timber, wondering the entire time if the next one had our name on it.

All we wanted now was to get back to base in one piece.

It was full dark when we returned to the deployment site. There was a little more activity now, some authorities and a handful of vehicles.

It was a relief being able to just keep driving. There wasn't much conversation. All of us had experienced fatalities before. No one felt like talking about this one any more than the others we'd seen.

We pulled back into base late at night, filthy, tired, and starving. Satellite news trucks were already parked outside. It's a four-hour drive from Seattle; they hadn't wasted any time.

The answering machine at the base was filled with messages. The initial news reports mistakenly said jumpers had been killed, and everyone's friends and family were desperate for updates. Cell technology was not up to speed here, so it was harder to get word out that we were all safe.

I was in the bathhouse taking a shower when someone yelled, "Is there a Ramos in here?" A good friend had driven twenty-five miles to the base just to see if I was okay.

THIRTYMILE MARKED THE FIRST Forest Service deaths by wildfire since Storm King, seven years earlier almost to the day. Fire investigators started to unravel what had happened literally before the smoke cleared.

The six firefighters who deployed on the scree slope had trouble sealing the bottoms of their shelters against the uneven rocks. Two of them actually left their shelters before the flames passed completely.

In most cases this is the last thing you want do, but here it saved their lives.

One of them, Jason Emhoff, wasn't wearing gloves. His hands were burning so badly that he threw off his shelter, jumped up, and ran. He hid behind a boulder for a few minutes and then struggled down to the road and climbed inside the crew van.

The second survivor, a squad boss, came down off the rock scree, sprinted across the road, and jumped in the river. He eventually was joined by the ten people who had deployed on the road. All of them had survived the burnover without injury.

The other four who deployed on the scree slope died of asphyxia from inhaling superheated air. Three of them were young crew members, aged eighteen, nineteen, and twenty-one. The other was an experienced thirty-year-old squad boss with two children.

As verified by air attack, the Regulars had made their stand in the most open place in the upper canyon. Between the rocks, road, river, and sandbar, it was nearly free of vegetation. The safety zone should have been safe.

Instead, it seemed like part of the fire peeled off, made a ninety-degree turn, and aimed straight for them. In the spot where the six deployed, barely a hundred square feet, temperatures hit over 1,600 degrees. It was as if a rocket had launched directly over their heads. Just a few yards away temperatures reached only about 500 degrees—survivable, if barely, in a fire shelter.

Nobody knows exactly why it happened. Fire can be strange that way. The Hagemeyers' pickup was destroyed, but right next to it the Regulars' van only had its plastic license plate frame melted. Granite rocks cracked in the inferno while bushes along the road were barely charred.

It could have been much worse. The civilians we were

searching for were off hiking in the backcountry and turned up safe days later. Among the survivors, the worst injury was Emhoff's burned hands.

The Hagemeyers were especially lucky to be alive. Thirtymile was the first time three people had survived a burnover inside a one-person shelter. Welch's quick thinking, scrunching up to make room for all of them, saved their lives.

The Thirtymile Fire burned for almost two weeks and covered 9,300 acres, more than twice as much as the Libby South Fire. It took more than one thousand firefighters and $4.5 million to put it out.

The official Forest Service incident report detailed a laundry list of bad calls and mismanagement, everything from recalling the lookout in the hottest part of the day to not having a backup escape route or safety zone planned out.

The two critical mistakes, the report said, occurred when the crew bosses decided to reengage the fire after backing off and then did little or nothing to prepare their crews for a potential burnover.

They had over forty-five minutes to ready themselves mentally and physically—clearing a deployment site, getting their shelters out, figuring out what to do with the civilians. Daniels had been one of the ten who deployed on the road. As IC he was ultimately in charge, and he drew particular criticism for not being a forceful enough leader.

If it was meant to calm the waters, the report did exactly the opposite. One of its key findings—that the group on the rocks ignored an order from Daniels to return to the road before deploying—infuriated some of the survivors.

The implication that their friends were responsible for their own deaths was too much. The survivors held a press conference soon after the report was issued to present their version of events: namely, that Daniels had never given such an order. The Forest Service ended up revising the report and offering a variety of versions of what happened. One of the versions supports the original accusation, though in slightly milder form.

Daniels, who was probably out of his depth as soon as the fire started growing, ended up being the only fire supervisor to face criminal charges. Four counts of involuntary manslaughter were eventually dropped, but he pleaded guilty to two counts of lying to investigators, including about giving the order to come down off the rocks.

He received a light sentence of three months' work release. His firefighting career was over. It was the first time an IC had been criminally prosecuted for negligence on a fire, absent malice.

Those last two words are key. A bunch of people screwed up on the Thirtymile Fire, from top to bottom. But no one wanted anyone to die.

Fighting fire is dangerous. Bad things happen sometimes, no matter what you do, no matter how careful you are. It's a part of the job a lot of people won't talk about, or try to deny. All firefighters start out knowing there are risks and hazards in this line of work. To some, that's part of the appeal.

Many questions hang unanswered about Thirtymile, including whether deploying smokejumpers could have averted the disaster to come. As to whether the six should have deployed on the rocks, firefighters have been taught that bare rock can be a safer place to deploy than brush; there have even been cases of firefighters surviving burnovers in rock scree without shelters.

The question that overshadows all the others, though, is why the fire's fury aimed exactly at those six shelters. That, unfortunately, is unanswerable.

CHAPTER 14

THE NOISE A LARGE fire makes is impossible to describe. People compare it to a freight train or a jet engine. To me it's more of a natural sound, a massive one—part roar, part scream, mixed with waves crashing and volcanoes erupting.

You know how there's a difference when someone is just yelling at you and when they're truly pissed off? You can hear it in their voice—something changes.

It's like that with a fire. It starts off small and can be defused in seconds, almost like an argument. Sometimes it starts yelling, though, and if it keeps growing, we'll say "she's really pissed."

At that point nothing can stop it.

In 2005, another NCSB jumper and I were double-timing through brush on a fire near Lake Chelan in central Washington. Branches slapped our faces and the thrum of helicopter blades filled the hazy air.

The spot fire below us was already yelling, and it sounded like she was about to get truly pissed.

We came on a pulaski and a radio lying on the broken trail.

The only reason jumpers would drop either would be to lighten up. That, or they are moving so fast they don't even know they dropped some gear.

Either way, whoever left them must really have been hustling. I wondered what the jumper could see that we couldn't.

Eight of us had jumped onto the runway of the local airport. We were picked up and driven into the town of Lake Chelan, at the lake's southern tip, for a briefing. The fire was in the hills above town and was already threatening homes.

This area gets a lot of fires in the summer. Eleven years before, the Tyee Fire had burned 210 square miles. Another 235 square miles had burned in the past ten years. A record low winter snowpack had led the governor to declare a statewide drought emergency this March.

People were still hoping this fire season wouldn't be so bad, if only because there wasn't much left to burn.

It took us about forty-five minutes to hike up to the fire. At first it was business as usual, working in light fuels and timber with a good helo pilot and one foot in the black (the burned-out zone).

Then I got drenched.

Twice.

Getting hit with water drops is part of the job when you're working with rotors and tankers. With larger Type 1 ships, you better find a safe spot first: water weighs over eight pounds a gallon and these guys dump them by the thousands. They'll give a heads-up, but you still want to keep an eye peeled skyward.

We work close in with smaller Type 3 rotors, since there's less chance of getting washed off the side of the mountain.

Today was unusual for two reasons. The pilot was dipping out of Lake Chelan, a deep lake filled with glacial runoff that's usually in the 40s at this time of year.

For smokejumpers in the Northwest, being too cold is a problem more often than being too hot. At high elevations there can easily be snow on the ground until mid-July or even later. Being damp is the norm, not the exception.

When it's over 110°F and you're cutting line for hours, like some California fires I've been on, bucket drops are your friend.

On a hot day there are few things better than taking a running jump into a cool lake. Now imagine the water is near freezing and a hundred gallons of it is landing on your head. Twice.

The first bucket drop gave me goose bumps, and after the second, I was shivering like a wet dog.

I took a few seconds to wring out my gear in the lull as the helo refilled and came back on station. But it wasn't until that afternoon before I was feeling warm again.

We were starting to get a lot of rollout. Rolling embers can help a fire flank you or get below you, so we were keeping a sharp eye out.

I was working near another jumper when a rock the size of a playground ball came bouncing down the hill. Before he could move, it rolled right between his legs, trailing smoke like a meteorite. It was like something out of a Roadrunner cartoon—except if it had hit him, he wouldn't have popped back up like Wile E. Coyote.

He looked at me with wide eyes that said, *Did you see that?*

We went back to work for another few minutes before he

stopped again and shook his head. "I'm done," he said, and set off for the safety zone on a ridgeline below us.

It wasn't long before the rest of us were in agreement. We were starting to see extreme fire behavior: spotting, torching, the whole package. There wasn't anything we could do anymore. It was time to pull out.

The JIC radioed everyone to head down toward the safety zone on a ridge below. As usual, all eight of us were spread out around the fire: sawyers out front cutting, diggers cutting line behind, experienced lookouts up high.

Everyone started hiking downhill toward the safety zone at his or her own speed. No rush yet.

I was one of the last out. I came upon another NCSB jumper, and followed him along a game trail the jumpers ahead of us had found. We ended up in an area of high brush. Being surrounded by fuels is not the best place to be. Plus, a spot fire had ignited below us and was starting to push up the hill.

Air attack, flying overhead in a small fixed-wing plane, was calling the JIC on the radio, but he wasn't responding.

After a few seconds, I grabbed my own radio. "Air attack, jumper Ramos, go ahead."

"Jumper Ramos, your location?"

"Working our way down to the other jumpers in a safety zone."

"Jumper Ramos, can you give us your location?"

"Roger that, I will ping you a mirror flash on your next orbit."

We kept walking through the brush until I could hear the plane coming back around. I pulled a signal mirror from my chest pocket, where I always keep one, along with a compass, for quick access. I angled it to flash sunlight at the plane.

"Jumper Ramos, I got your flash. You have a spot below you. You guys need to keep heading sidehill. I'm sending a Type 1 rotor to keep that in check." The heavy helicopter would be dropping close to two thousand gallons of water to support us.

We could hear the roar of the fire below us and see some serious convection pushing up into the sky.

One second everything is fine and you're taking a stroll down a mountainside. The next you're completely focused on the moment and wondering *What the fuck?*

I turned to the other jumper. "Well, we got two options, dude," I said. "If we hang out, we're gonna burn the shit out of our Spam. Or we can push hard and get the hell out of here."

The air around us was filling with smoke.

The choice was clear: haul ass. We took off through the brush. When we found the discarded pulaski and radio, I stuck the radio in my pack and kept tight on the other jumper's tail. We headed across and up the hillside, with the fire below and behind us.

Amid the radio chatter and crackling flames, one sound stood out: the rumble of a sky crane, a Type 1 rotor. I radioed the pilot to go ahead and drop, we're clear.

Hearing the sound of thousands of gallons of water crashing to the ground is enough to give you goose bumps. The hillside hisses and small rivers appear out of nowhere, sweeping rocks and other blackened debris downhill.

These pilots are the best of the best. Many times I've given them my thanks and a handshake back at base for covering our asses.

We made it to the ridgetop in a matter of minutes. The other jumpers were already there taking a quick breather and discussing regrouping tactics with the JIC.

I handed the radio back to its owner. "Thanks," the jumper mumbled.

The choice to pull back on that fire was clear, based on decades if not centuries of collective experience. And it was still touch-and-go for a moment or two.

What if the options aren't so clear? If nothing else, wildland firefighting is a series of choices: whether to engage in the first place, when and with what resources; how to best structure the effort; and whether to bail or keep fighting when—not if—the situation changes.

These are all questions worth reexamining as forest fires get progressively larger and more people die fighting them. The worst year in almost two decades for wildland firefighters fatalities was 2013, with thirty-four deaths, including nineteen in a single incident in Arizona.

The climate is changing, more people are moving into fire-prone areas, and we're still dealing with the legacy of over half a century of total fire suppression. If there was ever a moment to rethink the big questions, now is the time.

FIRE USED TO BE an integral part of the cycle of nature. Huge parts of North America burned on a regular basis, every few years in some places, every decade or century in others. The resulting patchwork of burned and unburned areas created natural firebreaks.

Plants adapted to fire, and in places that burned frequently, they often came to depend on it. Some species of pine only release their seeds after a fire scorches their cones open. One reason the California chaparral is so flammable is the oil coating on the leaves of the plants—which also happen to have fire-activated seeds.

Fire fertilizes the soil with ash and helps seedlings sprout by removing old growth and letting in light. Animals and birds eat the new seeds and berries, nest in dead trees, and hunt in the open spaces.

After our twentieth-century experiment with complete fire suppression, we now have forests with twenty to fifty times as many trees as they did before. Flames spread more easily, ground fires become crown fires. Fires burn hotter and kill everything, even big old trees that used to survive burns with little more than scorched bark.

We've eased off on the suppression, but overgrown forests are only part of the problem. Now global climate change is heating things up: 2014 was the hottest year on record. In places like the western United States, that means drier fuels, lower humidity, and drought.

The effects on wildfire ripple out like lightning. The mountain pine beetle, for example, has seen its breeding season expanded by drought and warmer winters. The beetles have killed seventy thousand square miles of pine forests in the western United States and Canada in the past decade, more than all fires combined. It's one of the worst insect outbreaks ever in North America. Those dead forests are primed to burn.

If you follow the news, you know what all this means: big fires are back.

Granted, they're not the multimillion-acre monsters of a hundred years ago. Forests are more fragmented now, and we're much better at keeping them from burning.

But wildfires have gotten much worse even since the turn of the millennium. The average fire is three times larger than in the 1980s, and fire season now lasts ten months instead of five or six. Over the past decade more acres have burned every year, on average, than in any other decade on record.

Every year seems to bring new records. In 2011, close to nine million acres burned across the United States. (The average in the 1970s was two hundred thousand acres.) Arizona and New Mexico both saw their largest fires ever.

In 2012, 9.3 million acres burned, the most since we started keeping track in 1960. New Mexico and Colorado both saw new state records. The Waldo Canyon Fire near Colorado Springs was the most destructive (346 homes) in state history—until the Black Forest Fire in 2013 burned more than five hundred homes and killed two people.

In comparison, 2013 was a respite: only 4.3 million acres burned. The Rim Fire in the Sierra Nevada was California's third largest ever, at 257,314 acres. The "Golden State" should consider changing its nickname to "State of Drought": 2013 was California's driest year since 1885, and the year after started with the entire state in severe drought—as in 100 percent of the third-largest state in the country.

Some scientists are calling the ongoing drought that has gripped the West since 2000 a "megadrought." This is the kind of thing that comes along every thousand years or so and tends to makes civilizations collapse. Extended dry periods have been implicated in the demise of everyone from the ancestral Puebloans of the Southwest to Cambodia's Khmer Empire.

In the more immediate future, one Forest Service study predicts wildfires will more than double across parts of the West by 2050. And just as climate change fuels wildfires, the fires boost climate change by sending particles into the atmosphere and killing trees that would otherwise capture carbon.

It costs the government a lot of money to fight all these fires. That means less for things like recreation, research, and, ironically, fire prevention. Meanwhile, firefighters numbers have dropped by 40 percent since the 1980s.

State and local governments have to pick up the slack. Sometimes that means drawing manpower from unexpected places. California and Nevada use thousands of prison inmates to fight forest fires every year. The practice saves California alone a billion dollars a year, probably in part because they pay the inmates $1 per hour. A few try to escape every year, while others become firefighters after they're released.

One of the main reasons costs are soaring is because of where more and more people are building homes: the wildland-urban interface, or WUI. When development starts to creep into forests, chaparral, or other fire-prone areas, some of these buildings are going to burn. About 40 percent of the houses in America are in the WUI now, and it's being built out at three acres every minute.

I can understand the desire—who wouldn't want a home (or second home) on the edge of a national forest or overlooking a beautiful desert valley? The problem is that most of these buildings aren't constructed with fire-retardant materials or defensible space around them.

When the flames arrive, state and federal governments end up footing most of the bill for fighting and cleanup. WUI fires eat up about a third of the Forest Service's fire suppression budget now. So local governments don't have much incentive to do anything that might slow down construction.

It's money and politics—but it puts firefighters in danger. And in central Arizona in the scorching summer of 2013, it led to tragedy.

CHAPTER 15

THE TOWN OF YARNELL, Arizona, population 650, sits at almost five thousand feet in the desert hills an hour and a half northwest of Phoenix. On June 28, 2013, a lightning bolt sparked a fire on a steep boulder field west of town.

The small blaze wasn't fought all-out at first, a decision that would come back to haunt fire managers. Despite the efforts of thirteen firefighters backed by small air tankers, the flames spread through the dense Arizona chaparral of manzanita, juniper, and scrub oak. Days of 100-plus temperatures had left the fuels as dry as a dead dingo's donger, as they say in Australia.

About five hundred acres were burning when the twenty-person Granite Mountain Hotshot crew arrived on the morning of June 30. Granite Mountain was one of the few hotshot crews in the country attached to a city fire department (Prescott, Arizona).

They were a mix of rookies and veterans, full-timer and seasonal, married and unmarried, ranging from twenty-one to forty-three years old (the superintendent). A few years earlier they had visited the South Canyon Fire memorial and hiked the steep trails beneath Hell's Gate Ridge.

After a briefing on weather, safety, and their overall mission—to keep fire out of Yarnell, its suburbs of Glen Ilah and scattered houses and ranches of Peeples Valley—the hotshots established an anchor point on the mountains near where the fire started, sent out a lookout, and started cutting fire line. They were joined on the fire by the Blue Ridge Hotshots, a crew from the Coconino National Forest, who were assigned closer to Yarnell.

The area hadn't burned through in almost half a century. In some places, the vegetation was ten to twelve feet tall and too thick to walk through.

By noon the fire had doubled in size, with a mile-wide front and forty-foot flames headed roughly north, away from the most populated areas. Hundreds of firefighters and half the available air tankers in the country were already on station, and fire managers were requesting more.

Yarnell is known as a windy place; a sign at the entrance welcomes visitors to the town "WHERE THE DESERT BREEZE MEETS THE MOUNTAIN AIR." On the edge of the Sonoran Desert, it's also brutally hot in midsummer. The thermometer that day read 104 degrees at 2 P.M., when a weather report came in predicting strong downdrafts from a thunderstorm building in the mountains near Prescott to the northeast.

An update at 3:26 P.M. confirmed that gusts of 40 to 50 mph were on the way. In the dry desert air, rain sometimes evaporates before it hits the ground. These half-curtains of moisture called virga cool the air, which then sinks and spreads out when it reaches the ground, causing strong winds.

Sure enough, the wind at Yarnell picked up—and reversed direction. The fire had been crawling north all day. Suddenly it surged to the southeast, straight toward Yarnell and Glen Ilah. A mandatory evacuation was issued for residents as engines and crews raced to protect the town.

Eighteen of the Granite Mountain Hotshots watched the activity from a burned-over ridge on the fire's west edge. They were in the safest place they could be: in the black, with the fire moving away from them. Another crewmember was acting as lookout on a road half a mile below them, while the superintendent Eric Marsh was off scouting but in radio contact.

From the ridge, the hotshots could see residents driving out as the flames approached the town. Some texted their girlfriends or called family members.

Then for some reason they decided to leave the safety of their position and move south along the ridgeline, along a dirt track in the general direction of Glen Ilah.

As they hiked they would have lost sight of the fire over a ridge to their left as they stepped off the track and dropped down into the head of a wide gully where a ranch house was visible at the bottom.

Whether their plan was to defend the property, rest there, or keep going and reenage the fire—the most likely explanation—we'll never know. It doesn't really matter, because in the time the fire was out of sight to the hotshots, it sprinted ahead four miles and changed direction completely. It came back into view when they were above the ranch, and it was charging up the canyon towards them.

They knew then just how terrible their position was. They were standing in a deep box canyon, surrounded by boulders and tall, overreaching chaparral, with the only practical escape route blocked by an approaching wall of flames. At precisely 16:23:35 hours, one of them called in on the radio: "Granite Mountain Hotshots, we are in front of the flaming front!"

Those listening in horror on the radio could hear chain saws working as the hotshots desperately tried to clear a deployment zone. They only had a few minutes at most to burn and cut away as much of the fuels as they could.

As far as anyone can tell, everyone knew his role and carried it out. No one panicked. No one ran.

At the last possible moment they deployed their shelters, many close enough to touch. The fire overran their position at 4:42 P.M. It covered the last one hundred yards in nineteen seconds.

There was no way any of them could have lived. Temperatures at the deployment site reached over 2000°F, with winds strong enough to lay fifty-foot flames over almost horizontal.

The lookout, the only survivor, sat stunned in one of the crew trucks after he heard the news. He had only been with the crew for two years. When the cab started to fill with beeps and rings—calls and texts from crew members' loved ones, hoping they might somehow still pick up—he had to get out.

Yarnell wasn't a big wildfire. When it was fully contained on July 10, it had burned only eighty-four hundred acres and destroyed 127 homes. But it was the sixth deadliest for American firefighters in history. The nineteen hotshots were the highest number of paid wildland firefighters ever to die in a single event—although the seventy-eight firefighters killed during the Big Burn of 1910 would have been paid if they'd survived.

IN THE FIRST FIRE investigation report, the Arizona Department of Forestry said the disaster was the result of poor communications combined with a catastrophic fire situation. It emphasized that the events leading up to the deployment would never be fully known because there were no eyewitnesses left alive.

Nonetheless, nobody knew exactly where the crew was or what their plans were. They were eventually hidden by smoke and couldn't call on air attack for a retardant drop or directions to safety.

That's part of the story. But it doesn't answer the big question: why they left the safe zone at all. A second report commissioned by the state Division of Occupational Safety and Health offered one explanation. Among other things, it said, the Arizona Department of Forestry had "prioritized protection of non-defensible structures and pastureland over firefighter safety."

In fact, fire managers had surveyed Yarnell, Glen Ilah, and Peeples Valley the night before the burnover and decided they were "indefensible."

The next day nineteen firefighters died trying to do just that.

The result? A fine of $559,000 against the Department of

Forestry, including $25,000 for each of the victims' families. An appeal is pending.

It's true that no one will ever know exactly what the Granite Mountain Hotshots were thinking as they started down that ridge to their deaths. We can make a pretty good guess, though.

Odds are they wanted to get back in the fight. It's perfectly understandable. "Life and property" is our creed as firefighters. It's programmed into your brain from day one. It's what we do: we provide a service to the people of the United States.

No one wants to be benched. You want to be in the shit, to be able to say "I was there." That's human, the lure of action. It's like dreaming about making the winning touchdown or beating the buzzer with a fadeaway three-pointer. This game, though, can cost you your life, and that's the fine line: to dance, or to step back and take the next song.

I'm not making any judgments about their decision. They were taking a calculated risk and they knew it. I've done it myself, especially when I was younger. I've gotten myself in situations I never should have been in, ones that I look back on now and cringe. I've had crew members get so excited to get in the fight I've had yell at them to calm down, relax, remind them we're getting paid by the hour and we're all going home tonight.

There has always been an implicit understanding that firefighters have an obligation to fight harder when homes are at risk. Depending on the mission, if those buildings are empty, that needs to change.

And it is: after Yarnell, Lewis and Clark County in Montana passed a resolution explicitly saying that firefighter safety takes precedence over saving homes or structures. Other counties have followed its lead.

If that ranch in the canyon had been an elementary school, hell yeah, go down and save those kids. Otherwise a building is just a building. Life and property—but property second. It's easy to say after the fact, but it's something we need to drum into our operators in the field.

We're not fire shepherds or fire scientists, we're firefighters. Anyone who fights for a living knows you can't win every time. Boxers will get hit, matadors will get gored. The list goes on.

The more we understand that in the fire service, the better off we will be. We walk around with a false sense of security that some agencies pound in our brain: *If you just pay attention in safety class, nothing will go wrong and you'll always be safe.*

But that's not the way it always works in the real world. In my opinion, we should have continuing education and frequent, graphic reminders that show us what happens when careless or stupid mistakes are made, and things go terribly wrong—things that only emergency or military personnel would normally see. We all need to remember the fire service is a dynamic and sometimes hazardous occupation.

The Yarnell fire couldn't have just been allowed to burn. When you've kept fire out of a system for long enough, it's not safe or practical to turn around and let it right back in again.

One way to ease the transition is by selectively removing the most flammable fuels, like dense underbrush and insect-killed trees, through cutting or controlled burning.

Thinning isn't cheap, though. The Forest Service spent

over $300 million on thinning barely 1 percent of its land in 2013. Budgets are tighter every year. And if a fire is big enough, it doesn't matter if a forest was thinned or not.

A controlled burn is faster and requires fewer resources—as long as it stays controlled. In May 2000, a controlled burn at Bandelier National Monument in northern New Mexico escaped and turned into a forty-eight-thousand-acre blaze that destroyed hundreds of homes in Los Alamos and buildings at Los Alamos National Laboratory. (Luckily none contained any nuclear materials.)

Some people worry that "selective fuels reduction" could actually lead to more development in danger zones by making them seem less dangerous. It's like the idea that seat belts encourage more reckless driving.

Development in the wildland-urban interface isn't going to stop overnight. But local governments can look carefully at zoning laws and building codes, and consider raising taxes on homes in fire-prone areas.

We already factor in the risk of natural hazards like floods, earthquakes, and storms in land-use decisions. Why not fires? California's new fire hazard severity zone maps are a good start, used for guiding building codes, though they'll be better once they incorporate local wind patterns.

Crazy weather events are already starting to make insurance companies raise homeowners' rates. Some companies are even getting into the firefighting business themselves. In some parts of California, AIG's Wildfire Protection Unit will spray the homes of high-end customers with foam or fire retardant, before or even during a wildfire. They emphasize it's a "loss mitigation service," not a private fire department, but it doesn't sound that far off to me.

Homeowners should take responsibility for choosing to live in fire-prone areas. They should never expect firefighters to risk their lives without question, especially if homeowners haven't done anything to prepare.

Your local fire department will be more than happy to do a property inspection, test your smoke alarms, and much more. They should be able to tell you how to install an outdoor sprinkler system and clear a safety zone around your property, and give you a long list of things you can do to make your house more defensible before the flames are right around the corner.

In the end, it's up to firefighters whether or not to engage. In the fire service, at least in the United States, we all operate under a set of safety rules and guidelines based on lessons learned from decades of deadly fires.

The Ten Standard Firefighting Orders were created in 1957. They have been updated since then, and now range from specific (post lookouts, identify escape routes) to general (be alert, act decisively).

The Eighteen Watchout Situations, added later, are times firefighters should be extra vigilant: when they're building fire line downhill with fire below, when their overall assignment isn't clear, when they can't see the main fire, things like that. Even taking a nap near the fire line.

The "10 & 18" are the closest thing firefighting has to a holy scripture. They're drummed into us during training and often posted on station walls or even in the head, so we can review them while attending to other duties. I was trained at Kernville to know them verbatim; get any wrong during an inspection and you'd be hating life.

These checklists have saved lives. That's not debatable. Memorizing them isn't enough, though. Firefighters need to do more than just obey a set of rules. We need to know how to operate safely and effectively in intense situations.

People don't think clearly when they're tired and stressed, let alone panicked. Our minds naturally go into tunnel-vision mode and start to cling to plans, any plan, even if the situation has changed dramatically.

The Forest Service offers great classroom education and hands-on training. Instructors from the military and retired fire personnel teach things like leadership and decision making, risk assessment, how to work in collaborative settings, and understanding the difference between managing and leading.

We have very smart, highly educated people in the fire service, and many of them are not being used to their full potential. After the fact, after a fuckup, everyone suddenly has the fix for what went wrong.

Not enough attention is being paid to those who are trying to bring awareness to new, better technology and solutions that could help keep some of these disasters from happening.

And paradoxically, "back to the basics" is something we neglect every day in our profession: things like how to take care of personal protective gear, basic compass and radio skills, and first aid and survival techniques.

If you don't want to be a tech geek, fine—but don't let your pride get in the way of asking someone else how to use your gear. Try to learn everything you can and refresh your knowledge as often as possible. Be part of the solution, not the problem.

Hands-on training in the field under experienced professionals is especially important for new firefighters. Learning skills like mindfulness and situational awareness help you stay aware and adaptable—and in a dynamic situation like a wildfire, that means alive. It would be good to have classes on common sense and accountability.

They're hard things to teach, but critical.

One thing that isn't hard is giving people the best tools for the job. If the Granite Mountain crew had had some of the safety technology that is already available, who knows, things might have turned out differently.

CHAPTER 16

REMEMBER WHEN BEING CALLED a nerd was an insult? Now there's a supercomputer in every purse and pocket, and Silicon Valley is way cooler than Wall Street.

Tech nerd, gearhead, whatever you want to call it, I'm a proud member of the tribe. I'm usually the guy on the plane with the most gizmos. I love testing out new tools, textiles, anything that might make firefighting safer and more effective.

This isn't a high-tech profession. Much of firefighters' gear hasn't changed in decades. Sometimes it's fine to hold on to things that work, like the parachute or pulaski. But there is a lot of advanced gear already available or on the horizon that could help crews do their job even better.

When I was at Kernville in the mid to late 1990s, we were one of the few helitack bases that had mobile phones. We were always the coolest guys at the fire because we had those big old brick-sized cell phones. They were a great communications tool, but we didn't keep them very long because we had to pay the charges (two or three hundred dollars a month, plus insane roaming fees) out of our own pockets.

The pocket-sized phones were just taking off when I started jumping. Now it seems like every fifth grader has an iPhone, and you can get phone service if not data on most fires.

It's a mixed blessing. Being able to call and send weather and intel back and forth from the field can be a huge operational benefit, depending on who's on the receiving end. Cell phones can save your ass. They can also leave you hanging at the worst possible moment. We're still a long way from guaranteed connectivity everywhere, especially in the wilderness. In the meantime, jumpers are trained not to depend 100 percent on any devices beyond our arms, legs, and brains. Every piece of gear ever made craps out at some point.

That doesn't mean you should leave equipment or devices behind. Along with my smartphone, I jump with a portable solar system (powermonkey) to charge my gear and a compact point-of-view video camera like a GoPro. I also carry a portable weather station (Kestrel), a handheld unit that measures and records everything from relative humidity to altitude, barometric pressure, and wind speed.

Depending on the mission, I might take a night-vision monocular or a handheld thermal camera, which comes in handy when you're searching for hotspots during a mop-up. Some of these devices can pick out a single lit match on a paved road in full sunlight.

One of the biggest challenges on a fire is keeping track of people. Sometimes I carry a GPS satellite communicator that can send and receive text messages and trigger an SOS (inReach). You can send your loved ones a ping to let them know you're okay. In track mode, the party on the other end can watch your every move, which can be critical if you get hurt or stuck in a bad spot.

GPS tracking systems have been around for a long time—I've been playing with them since the early 2000s, and they're getting cheaper every day. You can walk into Walmart and buy a tracking collar for your hunting dog for under $200.

Some people hear the words *tracking system* and think Big Brother. Nevertheless, the technology can be a lifesaver in certain situations. When a fire grows quickly from a small blaze to a large, complex conflagration, its command structure also changes, from initial attack to extended attack. The IC can become overloaded and may not always know where all the resources and personnel are located. GPS trackers would let the IC know the locations of the Type 1 and 2 crews that are already on scene.

The government already mandates a type of global positioning system (GPS) called Automatic Flight Following for aircraft. On fires, jumpers call it "Tanker TV" and use it to see who's in the air, where assets are, and what's going where.

Some departments thinking outside the box are beginning to use trackers already. The Orlando district of the Florida Forest Service was the first in the country to put GPS trackers on its bulldozers and fire engines after two veteran bulldozer operators were killed in a burnover in 2011. Their vehicles became hung up on stumps and they couldn't be rescued in time.

Now the agency is equipping vehicles across the state with GPS receivers and radio transmitters. Florida state officials say this "asset tracker system" lets supervisors see a vehicle's location, speed, and direction on a laptop up to two miles away. It's not dependent on cellular or Internet connection and only cost about $2 million—a small price to pay to ensure drivers are safe. This is starting to take hold in other agencies as well. I was a guest speaker last year in a safety meeting at the Forest Service in Flagstaff, Arizona, and proud to see a local employee there had done the research and purchased a few personal tracking systems to use for their crews.

GPS receivers are getting better and better at getting a signal even under dense tree canopies and rugged terrain. Working with some of the leading companies, I've been able to field-test new units that work even in the worst terrain we encounter. Still not perfect, but far better than what we had years ago.

Imagine if the location of all crews at Yarnell had been visible to overhead on the fire.

THE ONE PIECE OF gear a firefighter depends on above all the rest is his or her emergency fire shelter. The ones we're issued are better than nothing, but as I've explained, they still aren't nearly good enough.

A former aerospace engineer named Jim Roth is trying to fix that. Jim's younger brother Roger, a McCall jumper, was one of four people who died at Storm King inside a fully or partially deployed shelter.

One of the last times they were together, Roger showed his brother a fire shelter for the first time. "I said, man, whatever you do, don't trust that thing," Jim says. "It sounds like a death trap."

After the fire, Jim Roth was frustrated by the MTDC's lack

of hard data on shelter performance. He decided to start his own company, Storm King Mountain Technologies, to invent a better one.

When the Forest Service put out its call for new designs, Roth presented four prototypes that he and his team of volunteer experts had created. They were all lighter than the old ones, cost the same, and could withstand 2,000 degrees of direct heat. The National Interagency Fire Center and Forest Service went with an MTDC design anyway.

Roth kept working, experimenting with new materials that can withstand up to 3,000 degrees. His latest design is more angular than the jellybean-shaped New Generation shelter, designed to trap more air inside. It's also much faster to deploy, folded in a way that makes it pop open almost like pulling a rip cord on a parachute.

Roth is having the design tested under laboratory and actual field conditions. (Fire shelters, incidentally, are one of the few pieces of gear the National Fire Protection Agency hasn't set a performance-based standard for, but that's another issue.) His goal is to have a shelter than can withstand 2,000 degrees while staying 200 degrees or less on the inside for two minutes, all with a weight of two pounds (half the weight or those we carry today).

That's a generous margin of error. Most burnovers are over much faster; flames that are moving too fast to outrun at least pass quickly. At Yarnell, the flame front probably blew over the deployment site in twelve seconds or less. The problem is, the hotshots' shelters came apart in the first few seconds.

Not every burnover is survivable in a shelter. At Thirtymile, temperatures on the rock slope were probably lethal for close to an hour. There's still a big gap between conditions firefighters encounter on a regular basis and what our standard fire shelters can withstand. That's why I'm helping Jim with the crowdfunding side of his project.

Roth's shelter should be ready for direct sales in time for the 2016 fire season. Firefighters (or their loved ones) can decide if they want to buy them.

It's like when the families of soldiers in combat zones buy ballistic vests and send them over because the government-supplied armor isn't enough. Except in this case there's an extra hitch: technically a firefighter can't carry a shelter on a federal fire until it gets approved by the MTDC. It's going to be up to the firefighting community to fight for the right to carry a better, more protective fire shelter.

Firefighters have used signal mirrors forever, but they only work during the day. A laser flare works anytime.

Halfway between a laser pointer and a light saber, these babies are visible for up to thirty miles at night in optimum conditions, and one to five miles during the day.

The one I use, made by Greatland Laser, was designed by an Alaskan air tanker pilot. It has been used successfully as an SOS device and is highly regarded by search-and-rescue pros.

Never trust a piece of gear until it performs in real-world conditions. I've used my laser flare to guide jumpers back to camp when their GPS units weren't receiving.

On one fire I was on, air attack wanted to know our location but the IC was having no luck signaling them with a mirror, even in broad daylight, despite several attempts.

I double-timed it up to the same ridge he was on and aimed my laser flare at the plane.

"We got your green ping," the pilot said on the radio. I could see the IC looking at his mirror, puzzled.

"What the hell do you have, Ramos?" the IC said when I joined him. I showed him the flare and from then on we used it many times without fail.

The whole concept of air support has recently taken on a new dimension in the form of drones or unmanned aerial vehicles (UAVs).

I've flown remote-controlled aircraft for years and have become a big believer in their potential as a firefighting tool. They aren't the answer to every fire, but they can be an incredibly powerful tool in the right situation.

UAVs can see through smoke and detect the smallest fires using regular and infrared cameras. Compared to manned aircraft, some of which can cost thousands of dollars per day plus personnel, UAVs are huge money savers. Most important, they don't risk lives.

Plane-sized military-style drones have been used on fires as far back as 2007, when NASA loaned its Ikhana aircraft, a modified Predator, to Cal Fire and the Forest Service during the Esperanza Fire near Palm Springs. Fire managers used the drone's infrared sensors to map the fire's perimeter from forty-three thousand feet, to track its progress, and to send resources where they were most needed.

I'm more excited about the smaller models that are now within the price range of even casual hobbyists—especially the multi-rotor copters you see everywhere nowadays outfitted with cameras and GoPros. These are perfect for scouting: Are there any homes over that ridge? Are there people up there? A minute or two later and you have your answer.

UAVs can also be a huge benefit in tracking fires at night when other air support is grounded. They've started experimenting with this in Spain already.

With their internal gyros and GPS locators, multi-rotor copters can hold a position or even return to where they were launched when they lose the control signal. Planes and powered gliders are more stable in high winds but the copters are rapidly catching up. In the last few years there's been a huge influx of companies offering different kinds of UAVs that can take off, fly, and land on their own, controlled by software on a laptop.

The technology is there. The challenge is educating fire staff and the powers that be that UAVs are a tool that will increase safety and save money.

The FAA is still trying to figure out how to manage unmanned aircraft safely. During wildfires, they typically declare airspace restrictions to keep helos and retardant aircraft safe from collisions.

So far the answer to flying UAVs is usually no, but sometimes the FAA makes exceptions. In the summer of 2014, for example, the Washington State Department of Natural Resources (DNR) got approval to use them on the Carlton Complex Fire, the largest in state history, which was burning right in our backyard at NCSB.

CHAPTER 17

IT WAS A DRY spring and a hot summer in 2014. At the beginning of July, we had ten straight days of temperatures above 93°F at the base. On Monday, July 14, a dry lightning storm set off small fires across north-central Washington, concentrated in Okanogan and Chelan Counties.

Four fires in the Methow Valley, east and south of Winthrop, were immediately reported by residents. They waited for fire crews to come put them out, but even though NCSB was within shouting distance, the powers above had different plans.

Residents kept calling in smoke reports as the fires flickered and smoldered in the sagebrush and grass for the next two days. They started to grow.

Then they blew up, converged, and made history.

On Wednesday, one of the fires jumped the Methow River twenty miles south of Winthrop, burned the "Carlton Castle" to the ground in minutes, and roared up the Libby Creek drainage. (This was exactly the same route that the Libby South Fire had taken thirteen years earlier, just before the Thirtymile

Fire.) The entire watershed was evacuated in less than an hour.

On Thursday, the winds picked up from the northwest, following the canyon of the Methow River downstream to the Columbia. Gusts over 30 mph sent the fire, now two large burns, into overdrive. Between 3 P.M. and midnight it spread across two hundred square miles, burning an acre every four seconds. The speed and intensity of the run took almost everyone by surprise.

The tiny town of Pateros, where the Methow River meets the Columbia, was directly in its path. Police officers ran from door to door shouting for people to get out as fireballs rolled down the hills toward the houses. One witness described it as something out of the movie *The Mummy*, like a giant evil face of flames.

The power went out all the way to Winthrop, forty miles up the canyon. The scene was apocalyptic, especially after dark, when the air was thick with smoke and the only light came from the flames all around.

The fires merged the next day, becoming what's called a complex. Over the next two weeks close to three thousand people fought to get it under control. They threw everything at the blaze: seven National Guard Black Hawks, a DC-10 air tanker, more than a hundred fire engines, thirteen bulldozers.

By Friday evening, the town of Twisp was under Level II evacuation as well. Residents were warned that they might have to evacuate immediately and were told that if it went to Level III (i.e., get out now), there probably wouldn't be time for authorities to notify them in advance. Power, phone, and fiber optic lines were burned through for miles.

People were cleaning out the two supermarkets in the valley and driving the twisting road three hours across the North

Cascades to buy generators. Many residents had no electricity, phone service, or Internet. Only Verizon drove in backup generators to keep their cell towers going, earning themselves plenty of loyal customers for life.

Those who could still get online via Verizon were confused by conflicting information on the news and a temporary breakdown in official communications. Facebook became the only source of up-to-date information for most people in the Methow, even though not all posts were accurate.

We launched missions out of the NCSB base, driving to different locations and fighting the fire next to the road or hiking in. We call those missions "pounders." It's the same kind of work, minus the plane and parachute ride.

One day we overheard a radio call about a smoke report down in the valley that was being called inaccessible. We looked at our forest map and couldn't figure out why.

Two of us drove to where we could see the smoke rising from the side of a mountain and parked.

Inaccessible? Is this a joke? I took a compass bearing, marked our location, and geared up for the hike. A small out-of-state fire crew pulled up just as we were getting ready to head out.

"You guys are hiking in?" one said. "Our crew's not able to do it."

"Cool, no worries," I said, "We'll take care of it."

"You guys jumpers?"

"Yep."

We reached the fire in about an hour, put it out, and were back to the base before midnight: a perfect example of what two jumpers can do when others won't.

President Obama declared a state of emergency on July 23, by which time the fire had covered 390 square miles. Rain came the next day, but we were still seeing green alfalfa fields burn into August.

Over three hundred homes were destroyed. Luckily there was only one death, a man who had a heart attack trying to save his house.

The aftermath looked like something out of World War II: blackened hillsides laced with exposed game trails, bombed-out cars, chimneys rising from charred house foundations.

At the time of this printing, 196 families are suing the state Department of Natural Resources for letting the fire grow out of control. Many witnesses say their homes burned as DNR crews stood by. People would beg them for help and the crews would say they didn't have permission.

Both state and federal fire agencies, by their response times and actions, seemed to have had their hands tied by politics, at who knows what level. What emerged in the aftermath of the Carlton Complex appeared to me to paint a picture of jurisdictional hangups and issues regarding who owned what land, that prevented those agencies from taking timely and effective action. This kind of thing has been happening for years; they've just been lucky up to now. I've seen fire response times stretch from minutes to hours to days.

Our "inaccessible" fire was just one example. Leaders need to lead, not play politics. You need to put every available resource on fires that are in high-threat areas ASAP, like they do in some other states in the West. We should stop having so many jurisdictional disagreements and move toward more mutual aid and working together. Better to have the resources and not need them. It's crazy that high-threat forests like the Okanogan don't seem to have the same kind of protocols. Maybe there's some other strategy at play up top that we aren't privy to.

Could jumpers have kept this firestorm from happening, right here in our own backyard, by snuffing those four starts when they were still small?

It is the whole reason smokejumping was started back in 1939.

What I can say is that in my career we've only had to call for help a handful of times. Otherwise we've put out every fire we jumped. This shows the level of professionalism and success that exists across the entire jump program.

IT'S A LONG ROAD, developing and testing new tools and showing people what they can do.

I've always been fascinated by the idea that there could be a better tool, a better textile, a better way to do things. My dad always told me to buy the best—it won't fall apart on you like the cheap crap will. Even at the very beginning of my career, my captain at Riverside noticed my obsession with tinkering to improve things. I ended up being the equipment manager at the fire station before I turned twenty-one.

Over the years, guys would always joke that if you needed some tool or piece of gear and couldn't find it, Ramos probably had already been testing it for months. So it seemed only natural to finally get a business license and start my own company, Product Research Gear, LLC (PRg).

I call it a solutions company: we try our hardest to fix the problem, finding innovative answers to solve existing scenarios. We've vetted, evaluated, designed, and collaborated. We've taken things apart, burned them, pushed them past the failure point, and put them back together again. We've worked with some of the biggest companies on the planet in fields like tech, textiles and clothing, advanced medical products for field professionals, and helmets and footwear for wildland firefighters.

People ask me all the time why I have devoted so much of my life to this. I spend countless hours working on projects that I never make a dime on. But my answer is always the same: if I use something on a mission, or any other situation, I want something that actually works, all the time and under every condition, or at least as close as you can get.

Sometimes this is a matter of life or death. And that's what PRg is all about: finding the best of the best, and when it doesn't exist, working with the best companies to make it happen.

Jumpers tend to be old-school about their equipment. Pulaskis are tried and true, they get the job done. People have invented a few different machines over the years to try to make the job easier. Years ago, Francis Lufkin himself created a line-cutting machine, with the help of a machine company called Hofco. It looked like a weedeater with chains instead of string attached. He invented a line digger too. But neither really caught on, probably because of the limitations of terrain and the sheer weight of the machines. The pulaski is still the tool of choice for wildland firefighters throughout the United States.

There are two parachute systems used by today's smokejumpers, the ram air or square used by the BLM and selected USFS bases, and the round parachute used by most USFS jumpers. Each system has its pros and cons. The bottom line is to deliver the jumper safely to the ground

The system that works for us at NCSB is the FS-14. It's simple, even archaic—and has recorded exactly zero fatalities from not opening since day one.

That hasn't stopped the Forest Service from looking into switching every base over to the square, ram-air canopies that BLM jumpers use.

Parachutes can be a very touchy subject among jumpers. It's natural that anything you literally depend on for your life will evoke intense feelings and fierce loyalty. Some jumpers on both sides will tell you their system is the best, no question, because it's what they know.

Personally, I'm a round parachute fan. I've been a jumper since 1999 and it's the only chute I've used. So take all this with a grain of salt.

The ram-air is a great tool for certain conditions. It can handle higher winds than the FS-14. It offers more precise steering and in some cases softer landings. It's well suited to open places like Alaska and the Great Basin, which is part of the reason the BLM started using that system in 1983.

But in my opinion, I'm not sure switching every jump base over to square chutes is the solution. In my years of experience, I've seen plenty of valid arguments for both sides. It's not a cut-and-dried situation.

The ram-air canopy is basically an inflatable wing, so it needs a certain minimum forward airspeed to function. If you go too slow, the canopy can stall out and collapse. Round chutes don't do this.

Ram-air landings are softer, if everything goes right. If not, the canopy has a higher forward speed which could raise the odds of a rougher landing and maybe even an injury.

Before I started jumping, rumors had it that round parachutes always had the hardest landings. But after joining the program, I've seen a bunch of jumpers who routinely, seemingly always, land nearly as softly as their chutes do.

Mid-air collisons are a hazard no matter what chute you're on. When jumpers with round canopies collide they tend to bounce off each other, while ram-air chutes would more likely get tangled like a kite. But rounds can tangle too, and a collison a few years back ended up with a leg injury that later led to an amputation.

Ram-air systems do tend to have higher malfunction rates at both high and low speeds, most of which require reserve deployment. Injuries tend to be more severe with the faster canopies, broken femurs versus sprained ankles.

Three jumpers have died using the ram-air system since 1991, when a Missoula squad leader was killed when his main didn't deploy and he was too low to pull his reserve. No one has ever died from an FS-14 not opening.

Both chute systems have their own pluses and minuses. Instead of one solution for everyone, we should look at terrain and other jump factors and choose the right tool for the right job. Proponents say using ram-air chutes would let Forest Service jumpers land closer to some fires and get them out sooner. But in the Pacific Northwest, it seems pretty clear that our round chutes will allows us get us way closer to the fires here in the heavily forested, rugged terrain we need to land in to get close to the fires, finding small openings between trees that the round parachute can land in. I use a simple analogy: think of a plane compared to a helicopter. Which would you rather use to hit a tiny clearing surrounded by old growth?

The government loves to standardize things, for cost savings or sheer simplicity. But then there's the fact that the switch would cost somewhere in the neighborhood of $12 million.

And maybe the most far-fetched, I've even heard people worry that if the parachute switch does happen, and it results in more accidents, it could become one more excuse to shut down the whole jump program. The future of American smokejumping is far from certain.

I've mentioned the antijumper attitudes that linger in certain corners of the firefighting world.

To some, we're a colorful anachronism, like cavalry on a battlefield. Others assume we're too expensive, that we get hurt too often. Some assume that a situation might be too dangerous for us to jump, because they don't know how well-trained we are, how experienced, and how valuable the service we provide is. They seem to forget that we are absolute professionals on rough terrain jumping since 1939, and have helped train other Tier-1 entities in the U.S. and internationally on this specialty. We do know what we're doing.

In the matter of expenses, the average cost for an eight-person load of jumpers in a Casa jump ship, including two hours of flight time and a sixteen-hour workday—with hazard pay—is $6,500. Compare that to the millions of dollars it costs to fight huge conflagrations.

The average injury rate for Forest Service jumpers is 7 per 1,000 jumps—and only 3 of those are serious.

The bias can get almost comical. When Disney was making the movie *Planes: Fire and Rescue,* some of the artists visited the Redding base so they could get the details right—the details of the cartoon smokejumper planes.

When the movie came out, other firefighters started commenting on social media, saying things like, "Why all the attention on jumpers as usual?"

Seriously?

I know, what's the problem? But it is a problem if it affects whether or not jumpers are put to use.

If the people who make the decisions aren't familiar with and educated about what we can do, history has proven that we don't get dispatched. And we all know that "excess" resources tend to get cut. In other words, use it or lose it.

I've had civilians call me in person and ask why we weren't in the air. This happens to a lot of jumpers, in fact. Sometimes there are good reasons: maybe there's a hand crew on their way in, maybe the fire is in a different jurisdiction, who knows. I just tell them to call 911 again.

We're much more likely to be called to a forest where the FMO used to be a jumper. Nowadays some haven't met a smokejumper in years.

Some fire managers don't realize that we can jump close in or farther out, that we can land at an airport, that we can land near water, and so on. We're highly trained and have years of experience, enough to make the call about how dangerous a given situation is, and how to deal with the situation appropriately.

Jumpers are the Swiss Army knives of wildland firefighting. We don't just parachute into remote fires. We can also make it to close-in fires by helo or vehicle, often faster than anyone else.

We're self-sufficient for the first two or three days of an incident. All of us have some kind of medical training, often as first responders, EMTs, and even medics at times. All our aircraft are fully equipped with trauma gear so that we can help support search and rescue or whatever else is needed.

We can build helispots, drop supplies by paracargo, carry out prescribed fires, clear dangerous snags, clear trails, collect wildlife data—you name it. We're problem solvers.

All this is laid out in the Forest Service's *National User Guide* for smokejumpers. It's nineteen pages long.

If everyone read this manual regularly, we'd probably get called out a lot more than we do. The right tool for the right job.

Wildland firefighting has changed dramatically in the past decade. As fires have grown, the mind-set of fighting them has shifted too.

As more and more homes are built in the wildland-urban interface, fire managers are reluctant to send resources like jumpers to remote fires in case they need them later to protect close-in communities.

I've lost count of the times a fire we could have easily put out in its first few hours grew into a rager because someone "played it safe" and waited. Yarnell was a perfect example of that. Storm King too. And obviously, the Carlton Complex.

Once I was on my way to a boost in Silver City, a satellite base in New Mexico, when a tape recorder in my jump gear was activated by accident. When I played the recording later, I could hear the loadmaster chatting with his buddies as they put our equipment aboard.

They saw the smokejumper gear and started talking about how crazy those guys were.

Whether or not it's true, that mystique is something that can help ensure the program survives and flourishes. There's an institutional modesty—an understandable one—that make jumpers reluctant to talk about our work outside our own small world.

This self-reliance is a double-edged sword; half the time we fly in, finish the job, and leave before anyone even knows we're there. We're not heroes. We just provide a unique public service that we have become too reluctant to promote.

We need to overcome the insularity and let people know what we do. Because if we don't tell our story, someone else will. A few great books have been written by and about jumpers. Beyond that, there's not too much. Besides the film *Red Skies of Montana* back in 1952, there's Howie Long tossing axes in the movie *Firestorm*, a few made-for-TV movies, and various cable documentary series.

Jumpers aren't moving up into leadership positions as often as they used to. The old guard is dying out. Only a few of the Triple Nickles are left. Robert Sallee, the last survivor of Mann Gulch, passed away in May 2014.

Whenever I hear other jumpers wondering about the future of the program, I tell them, *Leave a legacy! Be part of the solution.*

This is especially important now that we're under a microscope more than ever.

Being a smokejumper is grueling, thrilling, tedious, rewarding, and ridiculous.

So why do it? With all the danger and drudgework, the headaches and hard labor, what's the appeal?

It's not the pay. Jumper salaries start at around $31,000 per year, depending on what government pay scale a jumper is on. We get 25 percent on top of that for overtime and hazard pay, which includes any time we're on a fire mission, jumping or dropping cargo—but not if we're just flying or on practice jumps.

It's definitely not the effect it has on our love lives. This job is notorious for the strain it puts on relationships. Dating a firefighter or smokejumper sounds exciting, and in the short term it often is. But the appeal of your partner being called away constantly to do dangerous work at a moment's notice, to who knows where and for who knows how long, quickly wears thin.

It's hard to find the stability that's so important to settling down and raising kids. Some jumpers can and do make it work, putting their shoulder to the wheel for three to six months a year and working other jobs and spending time with their families the rest of the time.

As any of them will tell you, it's not easy. Some jumpers will put in more than a thousand hours of overtime in a year.

Every jumper has his or her own reasons for wanting to join this profession badly enough to endure rookie training and all the rest.

There's the satisfaction of facing huge physical and mental challenges. The undeniable excitement of danger. The camaraderie, and the love/hate relationship that comes from depending on others for your life and vice versa.

There's the gratification of working in the most beautiful places on earth and seeing the real-world evidence of your efforts. Being able to focus on only one thing and escape the rest of the world for months at a time.

Jumpers aren't always the easiest folks to handle. Male or female, we're all alphas, and our training amplifies this inclination. The result is all chiefs and no braves, to paraphrase an old saying.

The lessons of smokejumping carry over into the rest of life. Facing danger, acting decisively, taking the initiative, sticking to a plan, having a fallback position—it's all excellent training for success however you define it. Jumpers have gone on to become top athletes, business leaders, entrepreneurs, professors, doctors, even an astronaut.

There's also the pride of being one of fewer than six thousand people to join a seventy-five-year-old profession.

For me it's all of the above, plus more that's difficult to put into words.

Not to get too mystical about it, but there's something about fire that touches something deep and hardwired in the human soul.

You know how easy it is to lose yourself in the dancing flames of a campfire. Now multiply that mesmerizing combination of beauty and danger by an almost infinite amount.

A forest fire at night or the ash-covered aftermath of a big burn is something out of another world. Smoky air shimmering with heat, showers of burning pine needles, embers shooting up like fireworks. The indescribable noise of all that energy being released as heat and light, a process that's older than life itself.

There's a reason the ancients considered fire one of the four elements.

I took two oaths in my career as a firefighter, one for the State of California and one for the U.S. Forest Service. For the latter, I stood and raised my right hand and recited these words aloud:

I, Jason Anthony Ramos, do solemnly swear that I will support and defend the Constitution of the United States against all enemies, foreign and domestic;

that I will bear true faith and allegiance to the same;

that I take this obligation freely, without any mental reservation or purpose of evasion; and that I will well and faithfully discharge the duties of the office on which I am about to enter.

So help me God.

It's an honor to carry on a long tradition of public service, helping make this country I love a better place. Public service is something I think everyone should do at some point, no matter how big or small the effort. As my dad always said, "Do something, son."

Every time I find myself standing in the doorway of a plane, getting ready to commute to work by parachute, facing all the unknowns in the air and down there on the ground, I'm sure of one thing: it's not just a privilege but an honor to have offered my service, alongside all the others past and present, as United States smokejumper.

> *The fear of death follows from the fear of life. A man who lives fully is prepared to die at any time.*
>
> MARK TWAIN

ACKNOWLEDGMENTS

Keep away from people who try to belittle your
ambitions. Small people always do that, but the really
great make you feel that you, too, can become great.

MARK TWAIN

First and foremost I would like to thank my mom and dad, my family and relatives for all they have done for me.

Thank you to my mentors and advisors—you know who you are—you believed in me and called me out many times: "When are you going to take off your Peter Pan shoes and get your ass to work?"—without you there'd be no PRg or book at all.

It's been a true honor to work for the United States Forest Service, and I thank you sincerely for all the opportunities and responsibilities you have given me along the way. I would like to also thank Menifee Volunteer Fire Company Station 68, Riverside County Fire Department, Olancha Station 6, Kernville Helitack 523, and most of all NCSB and all the smokejumper bases. To all the jumpers that I had the pleasure in sharing airspace with on countless missions. To the ace pilots, air attack, lead planes, tankers and rotors I've had the pleasure of working with—I'm indebted to you all. Last but not least to all the dispatchers and lookout towers throughout the United States. Thank you.

Special thanks to my editor, Peter Hubbard, who took the time to research the smokejumper program and contact me directly, and big thanks also to Nick, Katie, and the rest of the William Morrow/HarperCollins team. Julian Smith, for all your hard work, creativity, and dedication to making this happen. It's been worth it all.

Thank you to all my friends whom I have spent many days and nights with—from California to the North Cascades (freezing our asses off), to Baja California and across the Pacific to Hawaii. From eating like kings on the Sea of Cortez to getting our asses kicked during fire season, I'm truly honored to have you all in my corner and look forward to many more adventures.

To all the pioneers of the jump program from 1939 to date, and also the 101st Airborne, 82nd and the 555th Triple Nickles . . . Airborne!

For all the Tier 1 guys I have met along the way, for your friendship and the guidance you've given me—I have no words. Without you we would not have this freedom I cherish every damn day!

To all the top companies who have taken me under their wing so that I could think outside the box, it's an honor to be working with such excellence. Thank you.

Last but not least to my lady who put up with countless hours with me, late nights and early mornings and keeping this dream alive. Thank you for taking the chance and standing by my side.

To all my Brothers, I will see you in the East . . .

Instead of cursing the darkness, light a candle.
BENJAMIN FRANKLIN

U.S. FOREST SERVICE TEN STANDARD
FIREFIGHTING ORDERS

1. Keep informed on fire weather conditions and forecasts.
2. Know what your fire is doing at all times.
3. Base all actions on current and expected behavior of the fire.
4. Identify escape routes and safety zones, and make them known.
5. Post lookouts when there is possible danger.
6. Be alert. Keep calm. Think clearly. Act decisively.
7. Maintain prompt communications with your forces, your supervisor, and adjoining forces.
8. Give clear instructions and insure they are understood.
9. Maintain control of your forces at all times.
10. Fight fire aggressively, having provided for safety first.

Source: National Wildfire Coordinating Group

EIGHTEEN WATCHOUT SITUATIONS

1. Fire not scouted and sized up.
2. In country not seen in daylight.
3. Safety zones and escape routes not identified.
4. Unfamiliar with weather and local factors influencing fire behavior.
5. Uninformed on strategy, tactics, and hazards.
6. Instructions and assignments not clear.
7. No communication link with crewmembers/supervisors.
8. Constructing line without safe anchor point.
9. Building fire line downhill with fire below.
10. Attempting frontal assault on fire.
11. Unburned fuel between you and fire.
12. Cannot see main fire; not in contact with anyone who can.
13. On a hillside where rolling material can ignite fuel below.
14. Weather is getting hotter and drier.
15. Wind increases and/or changes direction.
16. Getting frequent spot fires across line.
17. Terrain and fuels make escape to safety zones difficult.
18. Taking a nap near the fire line.

Source: National Wildfire Coordinating Group

GLOSSARY

Air attack: The coordination of aerial attack operations over a wildfire with ground firefighting efforts is the responsibility of the Air Tactical Group Supervisor. Both single and twin engine fixed-wing aircraft, as well as helicopters, serve as aerial platforms for this mission.

Alumagel: a thickening agent used to create jelled gasoline, which is used in various applications to start fires.

Anchor point: starting point for constructing fire line, often a natural firebreak, chosen to minimize the chance of being flanked by fire.

Backfire: fire set deliberately to stop or change the path of a wildfire by consuming fuel.

Blowup: sudden increase in fire intensity or speed making it impossible to control directly.

Buckaroo: Americanized version of Spanish "vaquero," referring to cowboys and cattle herders.

Bureau of Land Management (BLM): agency within the U.S. Department of the Interior that administers one-eighth of the country's area.

Candling: tree or clump of trees burning up rapidly from the bottom; a.k.a. torching.

Canopy: highest level of forest vegetation, usually above 20 feet; also the part of a parachute that inflates to slow a jumper's descent.

Capewell: release system that allows a jumper to quickly disconnect harness from canopy.

Cargo drop: the dropping of equipment or supplies, with or without a parachute, from an aircraft in flight.

Chain: unit of measurement often used in fire management, equal to 66 feet.

Contained: wildfire completely surrounded by a fire line.

Creeping fire: low, slow-moving fire.

Crown fire: fire advancing through the highest level of vegetation, often independent of a ground-level fire.

Cubie: plastic water container for drinking and firefighting, available in 2.5- and 5-gallon sizes.

Deploy [fire shelter]: use of personal fire shelter for protection from flames and superheated air during an entrapment.

Deployment zone: area where personal fire shelters are used, chosen when possible for its openness and absence of burnable fuels.

Dispatch: command decision to move resources from one location to another, in a process overseen by a dispatcher based in dispatch center.

Duff: lowest layer of decomposing organic materials immediately above mineral soil.

Engine: ground vehicle providing manpower and water pumping capacity on a fire.

Entrapment: situation in which personnel are unexpectedly caught in a life-threatening position by fire; may or may not include deployment of fire shelters.

Escape route: pre-planned and understood route to a safety zone or other low-risk area.

Final approach: aircraft flight path in the direction of landing, cargo drop or smokejumper deployment.

Fire devil: spinning vortex of hot air and gases above a fire carrying smoke, debris, and flame, a.k.a. fire whirl, fire tornado.

Fire line: shallow trench dug down to mineral soil meant to stop the spread of a fire. Also "control line" or "hand line."

Fire Management Officer (FMO), also **Forest Fire Management Officer (FFMO):** individual responsible for providing leadership and program direction for the unit's fire and aviation management program; also responsible for coordinating the development of short and long-range fire management program plans and fire management activities on the unit.

Fire season: time period during which wildland fires are most likely to require organized firefighting activities.

Fire shelter: cover of metallicized fabric designed to protect one person from radiant heat and provide breathable air during an entrapment.

Fire weather: climatic conditions that influence fire ignition, behavior, and suppression.

Firebrand: burning fuel particles small enough to be carried by wind or gravity and hot enough to start secondary or spot fires.

Firestorm: exceptionally large blowup, often big enough to become self-sustaining over an extended period and consume all available fuels.

Flank: lateral margins of a spreading fire.

Front: boundary between two air masses of different atmospheric properties, such as warm and cold.

Fuel load: amount of burnable material in a given area.

Fusee: handheld device for lighting fires, a.k.a. flare.

Hand crew: trained and organized group of wildland firefighters, usually 18–20 individuals, who primarily construct fire line, burn out fire areas, and mop up after fires.

Heliport: permanent facility for helicopter operations.

Helispot: natural or improved area for helicopter takeoff and landing.

Helitack: use of helicopters to transport crews, equipment, and fire suppressants during the initial stages of a fire; also the crew involved.

Helitorch: aerial ignition device mounted on a helicopter that ejects short streams of alumagel.

Hooch site: place to bunk down for the night on a wildfire.

Hot spot: particularly active part of a fire.

Hotshot crew: a Type 1 fire crew, extensively trained and experienced, usually 20 to 22 members, primarily tasked with constructing, backburning, and holding handline, through the use of chain saws, hand tools, ignition devices, and water delivery equipment. They can engage in all phases of wildfire response, from initial attack to mop-up. They are also trained in specialized operations, such as hot spotting, spot fire attack, tree felling, and structure protection.

Incident Command System (ICS): standardized emergency management system to address incidents of varying sizes and severity, managed by an Incident Commander (IC).

Initial attack (IA): preplanned early response to a wildfire that may include sizing up, patrolling, monitoring, holding actions or suppression.

Jump list: list of smokejumpers by name that dictates jump order.

Jump spot: selected landing area for smokejumpers.

Jumper in charge (JIC): first jumper out of the plane and subsequently, Incident Commander of the mission.

Ladder fuels: flammable materials that let fire climb from the ground into the crowns of shrubs or trees.

Loft: part of a jump base where parachutes are maintained and repaired and smokejumper gear is manufactured.

Lookout: trained observer tasked with recognizing and anticipating changes in wildland fire behavior.

McLeod: firefighting hand tool with a hoe or cutting tool on one side and a rake on the other.

Missoula Technology and Development Center (MTDC): U.S. Forest Service research and development facility for public land management, focused (among other things) on developing and testing new firefighting equipment. (Formerly, Missoula Equipment Development Center [MEDC]).

Mop up: final stage of wildfire suppression, which includes extinguishing burning material, cutting down snags, and trenching logs to prevent rolling.

National Interagency Fire Center (NIFC): federal facility in Boise, Idaho, that coordinates mobilization of resources for wildland fire incidents throughout the country.

Nomex: trade name for a fire resistant synthetic material, (generic name Aramid) used to make flight suits, pants, and shirts used by firefighters.

On final: aircraft flight path suitable for smokejumpers to deploy.

On scene: emergency equipment or aircraft that has reached a wildfire location.

On station: emergency aircraft flying above an wildfire incident.

Overhead: supervisory firefighting personnel, including incident commanders, command staff, unit leaders, and others.

Pack test: one standard for determining firefighter physical fitness, consisting of walking a specified distance within a certain period of time while carrying a weighted pack.

Paracargo: supplies dropped from an aircraft by parachute or free fall.

Parachute landing fall (PLF): controlled roll designed to minimize the chance of injury during a parachute landing roll.

Personal gear (PG) bag: small bag containing personal items carried by firefighters.

Pounder: incident response by ground vehicle.

Pulaski: firefighting hand tool with an axe on one side and an adze on the other.

Ram-air: BLM smokejumpers use a "ram-air parachute," which is a rectangular, pressurized fabric airfoil, rather than the traditional round parachute used by the Forest Service.

Rappel: descending a rope using a mechanical device to control descent; called "let down" when descending from a tree.

Retardant: substance or chemical agent that reduces the flammability of combustible material.

Rookie: first-year smokejumper.

Safety zone: area cleared of flammable materials available as a protected space for firefighters.

Sawyer: chain saw operator; a.k.a. faller.

Slash: flammable debris left over from weather events, construction, logging, or other land clearing.

Smokejumper: wildland firefighter who parachutes into a remote area to combat wildfires.

Snag: standing dead tree.

Snookie: second-year smokejumper.

Spot fire: fire ignited outside the perimeter of the main fire by a firebrand.

Spotter: individual responsible for selecting drop target and supervising all aspects of deployment in smokejumping, rappelling, and paracargo operations.

Streamer: long pieces of weighted crepe paper thrown from jump planes before jumping to determine wind drift and descent time.

Swamper: worker who assists fallers or sawyers by clearing away cut material and carrying supplies.

Tango union: inoperable, broken.

Tanker: aircraft used in fire suppression.

Tower: Parachute simulation tower used in jumper training.

Two-manner: A small mission that can be handled by two jumpers.

Widow-maker: loose snag or tree limb in danger of falling on anyone beneath it.

INDEX

"Jason Ramos's *Smokejumper* is a rousing personal adventure story, a nutshell history of the great wildland fires, and insider's brief for making smokejumpers more relevant on today's fire line."

—JOHN N. MACLEAN, *author of* FIRE ON THE MOUNTAIN

"In a humble and interesting way, Jason Ramos takes us through his story of a young man aspiring to become a smokejumper. The reader joins him on his time as a volunteer urban firefighter, to wildland firefighting and training, to becoming a rookie smokejumper. During his adventures on fires throughout the west, interwoven in his exciting adventures Jason educates the reader about the other firefighting resources, the art of firefighting, the smokejumper culture, and lifestyle and human tragedies associated with his twenty-six-year firefighting career."

—BILL MOODY, *NCSB Jumper and Base Manager (retired) '57–'89, currently seasonal Air Tactical Group Supervisor and Aerial Fire Suppression Consultant*

"Jason Ramos, veteran U.S. Forest Service smokejumper, tells of nature at its most savage, of 2,000-degree heat and hurricane-force drafts, of heroic, sometimes lethal efforts to save the lives of people less prepared.

From a career committed to places and events few people see, Ramos delivers a frank, firsthand account of frontline—and behind-the-lines—challenges. Here you'll meet the people who fly between Heaven and Hell. And jump."

—WAYNE VAN ZWOLL, PHD, *former Special Projects Editor, Intermedia Outdoors*